SKY DOG
RANCH

DEDICATION

*This book is dedicated to the very first beautiful "boy" we saved
at Skydog Sanctuary, Jackson.*

*Jackson was an utterly incredible horse, and everyone who met him
fell deeply for this sixteen-hand hunk of love and kindness. He taught
us so so much about wild horses and, with his guidance and wisdom,
did a lot to make our sanctuary a success.*

*When he passed away, our hearts were shattered, but I still strongly
feel his presence and spirit watching over us all.*

*Some horses leave extra-large hoofprints in your heart when they leave,
and his are felt so deeply. We will never forget you, Jackson, and you
were the bestest boy. Long may your memory live on at Skydog.*

This book is for you. x

PAGE 1: *Huckleberry* • PREVIOUS SPREAD: *Cruiser and family* • ABOVE: *Jackson* • OVERLEAF: *Blaze and family*

THE WILD BOYS OF SKYDOG

CLARE STAPLES
Founder of Skydog Ranch & Sanctuary

with photography by Scott Wilson, Shannon Phifer & Jamie Baldanza

Additional photographs by Janelle Hight

T

TRAFALGAR
SQUARE

TABLE OF CONTENTS

FOREWORD
by Scott Wilson

CLARE AND I BOTH TOOK A LEAP OF FAITH when I first visited Skydog, not really knowing where we'd land, but trusting the personal journeys and shared love of wild horses that brought us together at the model sanctuary she has created to provide removed and rejected Mustangs with a second chance at life in the wild. And Skydog really is a wilderness.

It is a sprawling, rugged landscape, dominated by an imposing rockface, overlooking nine thousand acres of sage scrub, pine forests, wild streams, and a flower-filled meadow that breezes toward one of Oregon's oldest aspen stands—heaven on earth for more than three hundred recharged Mustang hearts, each with an improbable chance to roam free.

Of course, Wild Boys legends like Spartacus, Sinatra, and Commander will grab deserving headlines, but the renewed life afforded to so many misfits, injured, or otherwise hopeless horses is, for me, what really characterizes Skydog, and the tireless behind-the-scenes drive of its visionary founder to say stop: Every wild horse deserves a chance at life.

And love, it seems . . .

Just look at old man Read, approaching his thirties, who was rescued after years of dreadfully abusive handling, where his face was allowed to, literally, grow into his halter, leaving him with horrific collapsed nasal cavity injuries. Not only is Read now living—and breathing—freely in this lush, remote corner of Oregon, he has found new love in later life, becoming inseparable from his loyal leading lady. Now, that's an unstoppable wild boy!

These are the stories—and this wonderful book is full of them—that fuel my belief that with the right people in their corner, we can still save wild horses from the very system that was supposed to protect them. The collaboration—physically and intellectually—that went into the creation of *The Wild Boys of Skydog* is a crucial element

PREVIOUS SPREAD: *Driggs* • OPPOSITE: *Read* • OVERLEAF: *Goliath*

of that belief, knowing that good people and fine artists like Shannon Phifer and Jamie Baldanza will willingly bring their craft and ideas to a wild horse conundrum that is bigger than any one of us individually.

The majority of my own conservation and advocacy efforts in recent years have been focused on expanding sustainable on-range solutions that will reduce the pressure for removals and keep wild horses in the wild, where they belong. The beautiful part is, Clare agrees. Indeed, I have yet to meet a sanctuary owner, large or small, who wouldn't prefer to see their rescue services rendered obsolete in favor of an America where wild horses live and die happily in their natural habitat. Until then, of course, our gratitude for the care and protection our wild ones find across the equine sanctuary and rescue community is immeasurable.

It has been a joy and a privilege to participate in bringing this wonderful tribute together, with memories etched across numerous enchanting trips and the deep exploratory conversations that took place between countless pictorial gems, bound by a shared promise to reverse the fortunes of America's wild horses.

Their freedom, after all, is our freedom.

INTRODUCTION

IN MY FIRST BOOK, I opened by telling the story of how a girl from England came to start a wild horse sanctuary in the wilds of Oregon. It's the story of where my deep love of horses was born, how it flourished when I turned fifty, and how I decided to change my life entirely to one of service and following my passion. I feel blessed that I not only found my purpose and my calling, but I am also able to live it, which is such a dream.

This book begins with the practicalities of making my dream a reality for hundreds of wild horses and donkeys. It was daunting, but I already had around seven to ten Mustangs, albeit tame ones, and a handful of burros. I reasoned that if I could take care of that many, I could take care of more and that each one would be my teacher to help me help more. Somehow, I had a deep-seated belief that the universe would aid me in this quest to care for the horses, and my intentions were clear and pure: save as many lives as I could and then look after them with the highest standard of care.

With so many branded BLM Mustangs in need, where to start became the first question. My team and I decided to start with those most in need: wild horses who had landed in the slaughter pipeline. At seedy backstreet livestock auctions, kill buyers purchase and then flip cheap horses to make money off them before the horses head to their eventual fate of being shipped across our borders to be killed.

Many of the horses we save from kill pens have as many as three to five auction stickers of various colors stuck to their butts with the strongest super glue imaginable, which often means cutting off the hair they are stuck to. But in that moment, we transform them from a number to a name that we give them, and their new life begins. Taking those auction stickers off became one of the most satisfying tasks of the first few months of our new venture, or adventure, as it certainly became once we walked into the Wild Wild West of horse trading.

OPPOSITE: *Clare and Rebel*

Auctions seemed like a good place to start, and the horses we saved in those early days had the added advantage of being tame enough to handle for hoof care and vet treatments. I started off at my ranch in Calabasas, California, and then when I met my husband, Chris, moved to our ten-acre ranch in Malibu, where I could help more horses. Then I began my search for the place most of the wild horses we saved now call home. Previously known as the Nye Ranch, we renamed it Skydog Ranch after a Blackfoot legend about the first horses seen by the Blackfoot people. The chief told his frightened braves that the horses were sent by the old man in the sky to help them, like the elk and the buffalo, and named them Spirit Dogs or Sky Dogs. I loved the name and the idea behind it.

We began looking for land for the horses in Southern California and realized how expensive it was, so we moved our search to Central and then Northern California and eventually crossed the border to a state I didn't know, Oregon. When we first saw the ranch that was to become Skydog, it was in the middle of a snow blizzard, and we drove around, barely able to see the landmarks pointed out by our real estate agent, Jim Coon. I do remember Jim telling us how much water there was on the land and that water was the new gold, which stuck with me, as we were experiencing drought down in California. I figured that with water and forage, the land would be ideal for wild horses.

Although Jim thought he would never see the crazies from California again, I was back in spring and again in summer to make sure it was ideal. We put in our offer, and it was accepted. On the day I got the call, I was standing at Black Hills Wild Horse Sanctuary in South Dakota, where I had gone to visit Read, a wild horse with a terrible halter injury who we had saved from the slaughter pipeline. I was standing in the middle of some willow teepee

ABOVE: *Clare with Huckleberry*

sticks—I still have the photograph taken by Marlene Dodge—when I heard the happy news.

I saved the first seven horses before we had even officially closed on the Oregon ranch property. They began their journey with me in Calabasas before moving on to our incredible property in Oregon near Bend.

I remember it like it was yesterday: Marlene, our hauler, arrived at the ranch early, and we loaded up some tame and a couple of wild horses and headed north to start our amazing journey. We got there the next day and unloaded these first few saves onto Skydog soil, which has become sacred to me in so many ways. It was me; my right-hand guy, Jon Kasik; my husband Chris; our horse trainer, Victoria; and another amazing guy, Adam, who had worked with us in Malibu. Jim Coon was there to video the first horses landing at Skydog and right then and there, in that glorious moment in

Oregon, our big dream had become a reality.

It was August, and those early months were all about exploring the ranch and settling the horses in. In that first fall at Skydog, we also rescued a handful more horses to head into our first winter with. We wanted to start slow and learn about the ranch and the way it operated and get the lay of the land, quite literally. Plus, we needed to find the right people to help us, adjust to life in Oregon, and meet the local BLM corrals staff to see where we could help.

It was hard work, but as we headed into winter, we were confident we had enough hay. We had been told that winters were pretty mild in Oregon, so we weren't worried. Summer seemed to last forever, and it wasn't until mid-December that the snow started to fall, and we were all excited. Until it didn't stop, and the temperatures continued to fall. Overnights were -15°F, and when

ABOVE: *Clare and Whiskey*

we fed in the morning, it would still be -7°F. It was hard to speak or smile, it was so frozen. We had everything go wrong that could go wrong with equipment and sliding off roads, but we always made sure the horses were fed and fine.

One morning I will never forget, I was out in Jackson's pen, and I heard the sweetest tinkling sound, which I couldn't identify, but it was like a magical sound of fairy wind chimes coming closer. I realized it was Jackson's mane, which had frozen into strands that bounced off each other as he trotted up for hay, that was making this beautiful sound. I was so grateful I got to hear that as well as see so many things that winter. Even in the crippling cold, I was grateful for nature and her incredible power.

When we started Skydog, so many people were excited, offering to come help and get involved in saving wild horses. I used to say to Jon, "We'll build it, and they will come," from the movie *Field of Dreams*, and I assured him everyone would help. One day, I turned to him with a balaclava on my frozen face and said, "Nobody's coming, are they?" It was a funny moment, but we had signed up for this and were determined to get up every day and face Oregon's

coldest winter in thirty-five years with smiles and do all we could to keep the horses happy and well. And they thrived.

We had some setbacks that first winter, but we learned something new every single day. When we weren't working for the horses, we were learning, growing, and soaking up knowledge from neighbors, friends, and local rescues who came out to say hello. We got our 501(c)(3) nonprofit status that Christmas, which was the best present, as we could finally fundraise to take horses without paying for everything ourselves.

I know how lucky we were to have my husband, Chris, fund so much of what we did to get started. He bought Polaris vehicles to feed hay, quads to ride fences, tractors, trailers, trucks, and salaries—pretty much all of that was Chris. I had told him that if he helped me start this dream, we would be fully self-supporting by year three. Amazingly, we made it within eighteen months of that promise, and the more people supported us, the more horses and donkeys we were able to save. And so we made it through winter, and the saving started in earnest. You are about to meet some of the incredible wild horses we saved over the past ten years.

ABOVE: *Bo and friends* • OPPOSITE: *Clare*

But it all began with a tall black horse named Jackson, whom everyone fell in love with at first sight. That beautiful boy, our first save, gave me every ounce of his strength and love to keep me going in those first hard months. Jackson will never be forgotten as the first Mustang we saved as Skydog and the first one to jump out of a trailer onto this land and hear me say, "Welcome to Skydog, welcome home." He and his mare, Lisa Marie, were from Oregon, and bringing horses back to their home state and keeping bonded pairs together has been one of the biggest criteria as we grew the sanctuary and had to make choices about who to say yes to.

The horses and what they taught us always led the way. They guided us and showed us how to do this through everything they told us, and yes, horses are always talking if you choose to listen. And through those first months until today I have felt driven and motivated by the strongest force, which I can only describe as unconditional love. It is an energy that throws me out of my bed every morning and guides my every decision and action through the day. It is based on one simple question: What is best for the horses?

With Jackson and Buddy being the first two boys we learned the most from, let's meet some of the other more memorable wild boys ever to jump out of a trailer in the past ten years and call Skydog home.

And there was only one horse who could start this story off . . . let's go!

OPPOSITE TOP: *Clare* • OPPOSITE BOTTOM: *Clare and Bo* • ABOVE: *Clare and Wilson* • OVERLEAF: *Horses feeding below Sheep's Rock*

From Despair to Freedom

ATSA THE GREAT. I had no idea when I got an email from Stephanie in Missouri that we were looking at a horse who would become a legend at Skydog. She told the saddest story about Atsa and his plight, and something about looking at this horse's lost and defeated expression forced me to help him. That and the fact he was from Warm Springs Herd Management Area (HMA), Oregon, a herd we had taken so many horses from after the roundup of 846 horses, 41 burros, and 2 mules in 2018. It was a particularly lethal roundup, leaving 32 animals dead immediately following the gather and dozens more that I was aware of in the couple of months following.

I still recall all the Warm Springs horses we've taken, from four orphan foals to mare-foal pair Grace and Sunshine to Chief and Hawk, as well as Charlie, Phoenix, and Ghost, and Elsa and her twins. So many horses at Skydog came from this herd, some immediately in the aftermath of the large roundup and some who ended up in the slaughter pipeline years later, like Rhiannon and Rose. So I looked at the face of this once-proud wild horse and knew we had to help him.

Atsa's adopter had hired Stephanie to work with him, ostensibly to train him to load on to a trailer to get rid of him. Stephanie did start working with him but then did the remarkable thing of asking to take him, to see if she could train him and rehab him at her facility. The lady agreed and Steph had trailered Atsa to her facility and spent several months trying to work with him and get his health back, as he had developed some horrible respiratory issues.

He had been kept and hidden away in a tiny pipe pen inside the barn, where his manure had piled up so high he had to wade through it to get to his water bucket or feed. This had caused his lungs to be damaged by the

OPPOSITE: *Atsa*

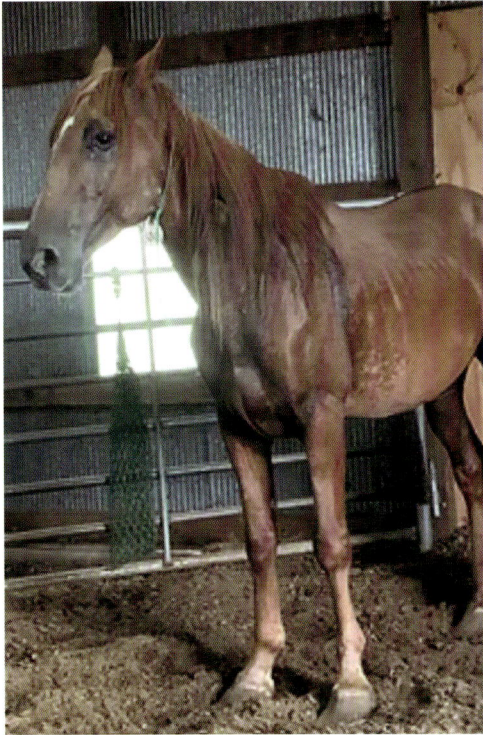

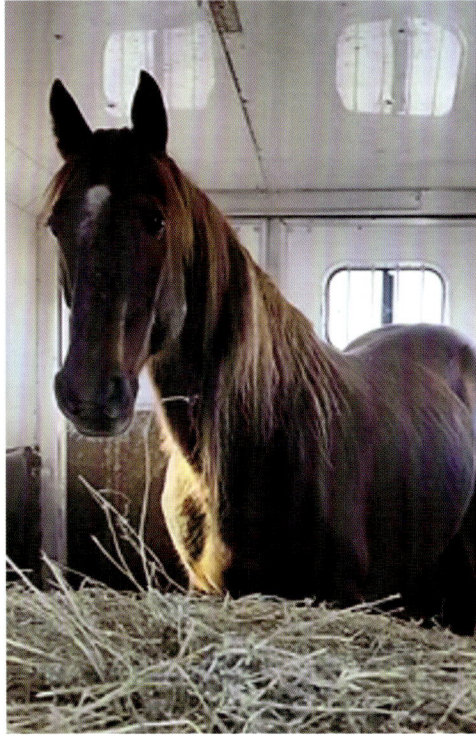

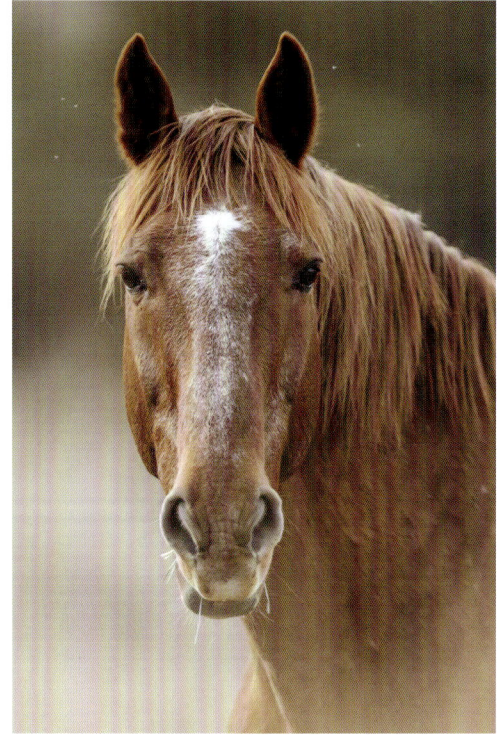

fumes from the manure. The lack of movement had been terrible for his joints, and the muscle loss was severe. But Steph continued to work with him and managed to get Atsa to hers and the rehabilitation began in earnest.

Atsa was utterly traumatized by human contact and was too wild to turn out onto more land, so he was contained in a long skinny run where he finally had fresh air, good food, and clean water. Little by little he improved, and Steph had the vet and farrier visit, who anesthetized Atsa to get his long feet trimmed and some vet care for him finally.

At this point, Steph reached out to us, and we are so glad and forever grateful that she did. We said yes, and that's how, on a cold snowy January day in 2023, we all stood in the arena at Skydog while Steph pulled the trailer up to the gate and opened the door—and then began the most painful and sad unloading of a horse I have ever had the heartbreaking task to witness. We were amazingly able to get a photo of Atsa on the range when he was wild and free, and it was one of the first photographs taken by photographer Larry McFerrin on the Warm Springs range. Atsa stood tall, proud, and majestic, so it was hard to believe that this shell of a horse I saw shaking before us, terrified to move forward and traumatized by the sight of humans, was the same animal. He felt safer and more secure inside the trailer than stepping into a future that he was sure would be more of the same.

Larry was actually there for Atsa's arrival, and he took more photographs to compare to his earlier ones, and even he was moved to tears by the sight. Atsa gradually shuffled forward with some encouragement from Steph and followed the little pieces of alfalfa she trailed down the ramp into the arena. We waited almost two hours for him to come out, and the second all four feet were on Skydog sand, we went to get him a friend who I knew would calm and reassure him. We brought Gabriel down into the arena, and they said hello, and we left them for a while. I returned and saw Gabriel and Atsa grooming each other in comfort and solidarity. For a herd animal to have had no other horses close to him for years was a terrible punishment, especially a wild horse, who relies on herd mates and family for psychological well-being.

The next day, we moved Atsa and Gabriel up to a small pen with Pegasus and Rocky, two other very wild and shy horses who shared Atsa's trepidation toward humans, and he slowly found confidence with new friends and a small band of his own. Gradually, the band grew in size when they were added to a pen containing four other BLM horses returned by trainers when they made it clear domestic life wasn't for them. At the sight of Atsa running in the snow, his head high and confidence returning, I could see glimpses of the horse he once was and would be again.

When the day finally came to turn him out onto the land with his group, it was triumphant to see Atsa lead the band as they ran down the dirt road to freedom and a new life. Since then, he has become best friends with Metolius, an extraordinary horse from Stinkingwater, Oregon. They spent that summer high up on the hillside in the skeleton trees above grazing, as far from humans as possible.

I don't know what makes some horses resonate with so many people who root for them and fall in love with the idea of restoring them to their former glory. For those who witnessed Atsa's painful and difficult arrival at Skydog, he captured their hearts, and they wanted to rid him of his fear. What so

many of these horses go through before arriving with us is heartbreaking but watching them heal and recover helps us heal along with them. Atsa was the most amazing conduit for people to first identify with his trauma and then to witness it melt away over time, inspiring me and many others to heal their own traumas and let them go, as Atsa had done so beautifully and bravely.

Atsa now leads a herd of incredible wild horses with a wisdom and strength acquired from having survived one of the darkest nights any wild horse could be forced to endure. The peace that now emanates from those once terrified eyes is a gift only freedom and wildness could restore.

THIS SPREAD: *Atsa* • OVERLEAF: *Atsa and his band*

skydogsanctuary

Atsa

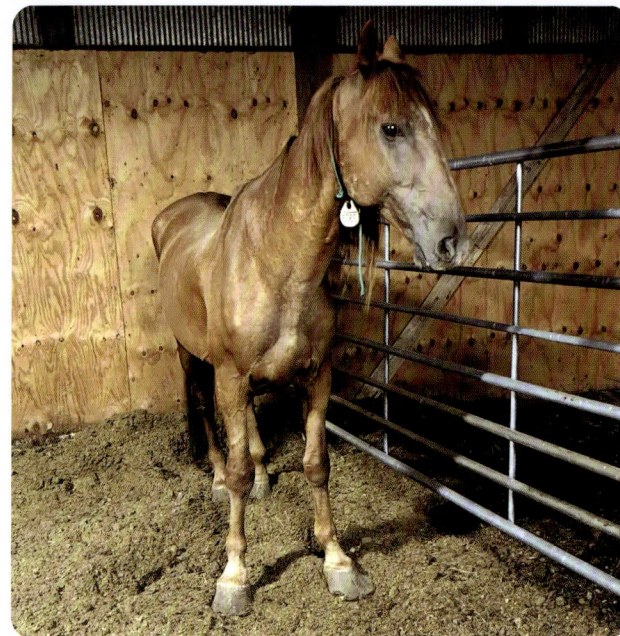

Welcome home, Atsa. We have been doing this for some time now, so we've met a lot of wild horses. Sadly, I've never experienced such a deeply troubled and hurt soul as Atsa. The trauma he's experienced since being rounded up and adopted has been immense. And it's heartbreakingly tragic that a once wild and proud stallion has been reduced to this terrified individual. Some of the backstory I heard from Steph was hard to hear and even harder to comprehend or bear. It took a long time for him to feel safe enough to come off the trailer and into a new space. It was such a relief when he did, and as his feet touched Skydog ground, I thanked the heavens for bringing him to us and for helping him survive long enough to get here. And now I have to shrug off the deep sadness I feel for him and show him he has a whole lot of life left to fight for. He's the tallest Mustang I have ever met, easily seventeen hands of chestnut beauty with a heart-shaped star on his forehead. That's probably what got him put on Internet adoption, his height and floaty trot. That is not the criteria upon which they should choose a horse for domestic life; they should try harder to understand the horse's disposition. He was aged at fifteen then but was clearly in his twenties, and if ever there was a candidate for sanctuary, this is the poster child. He's home now, and the healing begins in earnest. Seeing how absolutely terrified he is, we will go get him a friend to help him decompress. He traveled a long way from home just to make it all the way back. He's one of the lucky ones. I am sending so much love from my heart to his in hopes that he feels it and it reaches his heart. We have many of his herd here at Skydog, so I hope he gets to meet them and feels like his worries are over now, because they are. Beautiful boy, the nightmare is over and only good days forever now. ❤️

OVERLEAF: *Atsa*

2

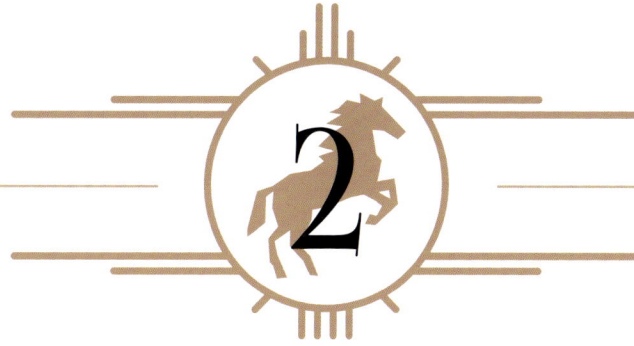

Miracles from Heaven

RANGO, WHO HELPED SO MANY HORSES, is one of my favorite saves in Skydog history. People often ask how I find out about the scores of horses we eventually save, and sadly, these days, I receive ten to twenty emails, messages, and tags a day about wild horses who need help. They're either auction postings, kill pen pages, of which there are many, or letters from owners wanting their horse or horses to come to Skydog. It's an overwhelming number, and the weight and burden of wanting to help them all weighs heavily on my heart.

So it was just another day when someone tagged me on a kill pen horse in Bastrop, Louisiana. A photograph of a battered bay Mustang, covered in bites and scrapes, emanating fear, wild eyes looking for a way to escape, hit me right in the heart. I looked at the photo and marked it to come back to. Later that night I was sent a screenshot of a Mustang Meg Facebook post identifying him as a South Steens HMA horse named Rango. I immediately sent the photo to Shannon Phifer, my dear friend and photographer of South Steens horses for years. She answered me back with a photograph of Rango in the wild, looking almost unrecognizable as the same horse. So sleek, fat, proud, and noble on the range, juxtaposed with this photo of a terrified, muddied horse in a small iron pen. My heart sank.

I knew what I had to do: bring him home to the land he loved and lived on for so many years and restore him to his former glory. I messaged the pen, paid a few hundred dollars for him, and called our beloved hauler, Steve Egner, who lives in Oklahoma, requesting a run to Louisiana to pick Rango up. He said yes, and so did our quarantine, Angela, who has taken in many wild horses for us and will hold them until we are ready to bring them to Skydog.

All the pieces fell into place, but then came a whole bunch of information I had never asked for or gone searching for. Shannon discovered that Rango had been part of a shipment of older South Steens stallions sent to a BLM Storefront in North Carolina. Two had been

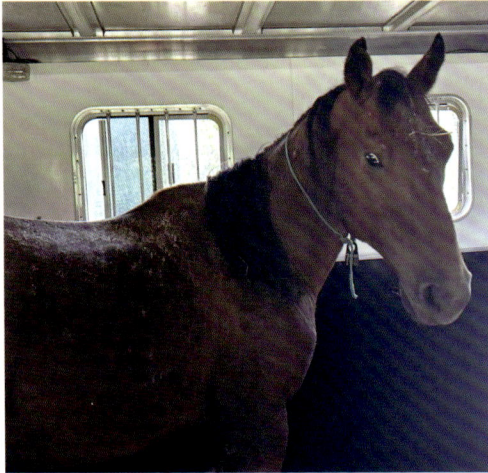

adopted out to a young girl for training, and the photograph clearly showed both Rango and another Steens horse, Commander, landing at her place as she had asked for help on a Mustang Facebook page, stating one of them appeared blind in one eye.

Sadly, we then found out both horses had been subsequently sent to a livestock auction in Knoxville, Kentucky. We found a photograph we had been tagged in by someone, showing them cowering in the corner together, both as scared as they could possibly be. A woman emailed us about having seen them there, how they were shaking with fear, and how terrible she felt for them. And suddenly, the search was on for Commander. We had to find him before he was shipped to slaughter from one of many kill pens that bought horses from that auction.

Caroline from Horse Welfare Collective took over the search, and she was relentless. She called the auction house numerous times and tracked down every lead about who was there that night and who might have Commander. During this time, when we were actively looking for Commander, Rango traveled to Oregon because he had cracked his skull open at the kill pen, and the open wound was showing signs of infection and needed immediate treatment. No vet close by felt up to treating him in what is essentially a cattle chute, so he came home for us to examine his forehead with the help of our vets at Bend Equine, whom we have worked with for nearly ten years now. The vet team came out to clean and stitch the horrible wound. He was put on a course of antibiotics, and he was healing physically, but sadly, the emotional scars were becoming all too evident.

Rango was one of the most traumatized horses we had ever encountered. He would snort and blow anytime anyone entered his large area in the Elk Barn. He would look around, his eyes

TOP LEFT & OPPOSITE: *Rango* • TOP MIDDLE: *Commander* • TOP RIGHT: *Ranger* • ABOVE: *Commander and boys*

darting up the perimeters, seriously considering scaling and going over the nine-foot wooden walls. He just wouldn't settle or get into any routine, and whenever he saw someone enter his gate, it was as if it was for the first time. His was without doubt the strongest fight-or-flight instinct I had experienced. It was heartbreaking seeing him so upset. There was no progress on the search for Commander, and it was then that Shannon told me about another wild horse named Ranger, who Rango had been lieutenant to on the range. He was at the corrals after being rounded up months earlier, and Kayce had even asked us to take him at one point, as he wasn't eating and had very few teeth to chew with, which he needed to get the calories out of the hay they provided him.

At the time, we hadn't said yes due to the horrifying attacks we experienced anytime we took a well-known South Steens horse.

But now this was an emergency, so we called the corrals and found out he was there, not doing well, and needed our help, too. It was a win-win. We drove to the BLM corrals to get Rango's old mentor and band leader and were stunned by this incredible old soul of a horse who was so calm under pressure and unbothered as he hopped on our trailer with no fear, not a flicker of worry. When he was unloaded at ours, he walked out of the trailer as if he knew exactly why he was there and what work he had come to do.

We released Rango with his stitches still in to save time, and to say that he transformed from a shaking wreck to the calm, confident, and self-assured horse he had once been in the wild is no exaggeration. He was a different horse; Ranger's presence instantly made him feel safe and secure, and because Ranger showed no fear of the humans, Rango didn't either. He took his cues from his trusted leader, as always, and he settled down.

And then the most extraordinary thing happened.

First, I received a message from someone who told me that they knew Commander had been bought by a guy who came to that sale every month and bought one horse to feed to his pigs. I almost threw up and was shaking with the horror of that and momentarily gave up hope that we were ever going to find Commander. Then, a couple of days later, Caroline sent me a simple text with three words: "We found him." After that, it was a blur of making arrangements, calling our quarantine, and getting his paperwork done to travel.

The crazy part of this story is that Caroline had tracked down the trader who bought him and tried to load him, along with other horses for slaughter, and they could not, despite their best efforts, get Commander on the trailer. So he remained, and the man said he would sell him for a thousand dollars, and I said yes. When we sent a trailer to pick him up, he got on right away—Mustang strong and Mustang smart. It was a miracle.

He stopped off at quarantine and then on to Skydog, arriving emaciated and scared but alive. He was sick for a while, but as soon as we could, we turned him out with Ranger and his dear friend Rango, and it was an incredible reunion. Our friends Zach Braff, Christa Miller, and her daughter Charlotte Lawrence were visiting that day, and they all filmed some of it. Shannon Phifer was also there and took incredible photos of the reunion of these three legends of South Steens.

The most heartbreaking part of this story is that a few weeks later, we found Ranger passed away on a small hill where he had laid down and gone to sleep. He'd had a long life on the range, a tough life where he fought hard for his family. He was then rounded up in his twenties and lost a lot of weight at the corrals due to having no teeth. Even though we had put at least a hundred pounds of weight on him while he was with us, I truly believe he knew his work with us was done, and he wanted to pass away with the views of his beloved homeland in his tired eyes.

Our vet examined him a couple of hours later and said there was no sign of struggle; he had just gone to sleep. It was a fitting end to the life of a legend who brought such peace to his old lieutenant, Rango. He left his two comrades with us to live the new chapter of their lives safely and together. We will never forget you, Ranger, and thank you for all you did for these two boys.

OPPOSITE: *Rango and Commander* • ABOVE LEFT: *Ranger* • ABOVE RIGHT: *Ranger and Rango* • OVERLEAF: *Ranger*

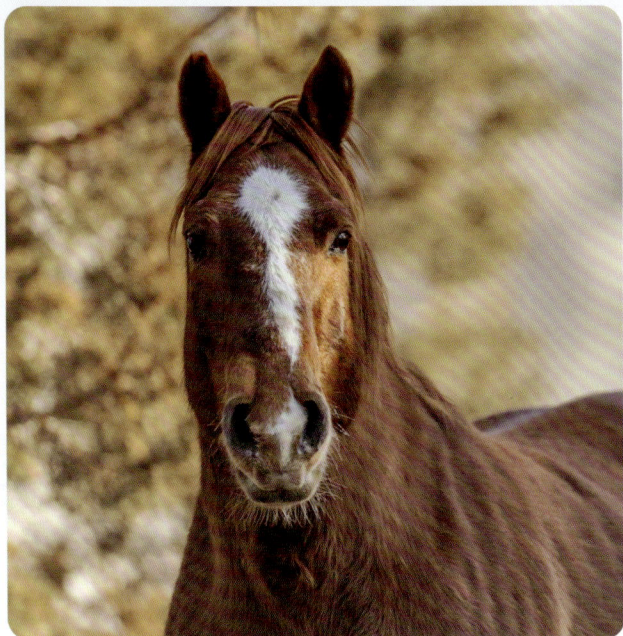

skydogsanctuary   *Commander*

What a good boy Commander is, and I wanted to say sorry from all of us for what he had to endure. This handsome boy has done nothing but eat and sleep and listen to every word I say to him. It's crazy to sit in the dirt and just watch him and send him love. With any big save that we do, the rumor mill works overtime to try and direct attention away from the utter disgrace of the entire situation, hoping to cause a distraction. And when they go low, we go high. We lead with love and truth, as those values have never let us down. It is love that brought Commander home, and it's all I want him to feel. Of course, these recent saves have been a bitter pill to swallow, witnessing what these once majestic band stallions have been reduced to and ending up in the slaughter pipeline "they" like to pretend doesn't exist. But I spent years ignoring horses from this herd because I didn't want to "draw fire," but then I realized that's what they want. To stop us from shining a white-hot spotlight on the horrors that happen to these horses after they are adopted or sold. Last year, we rescued over twenty South Steens horses from a notorious kill pen in Colorado. It doesn't matter to us if they have a name or not, and it doesn't really matter to our followers as they don't know the horses' names or stories either. All they see is a horse in need, who was let down by this broken system at every turn. You only have to take one look at this horse—his condition, his feet, his weight—to know who is on the right side of this story. It's the people who rescued him to give him his dignity and strength back. So throw all the arrows you want at us, but you won't ever stop us from saving a horse in need and giving them the best care imaginable for the rest of their beautiful lives. We can hold our heads up high, as will Commander. Doing this work is beautiful, and we get to go to sleep every night after working long days to care for the horses we have saved and the ones you wanted to dispose of because you couldn't ride them. Commander is home—it's a tale with the happiest of endings, and on we go. ❤️

3

Kill Pen Saves

FOLLOWING THE INCREDIBLE RESCUE of Rango and Commander, two South Steens legends, came another older Steens horse who also found himself terrified and being handled in a kill pen in Texas. They said he was from Oregon, so I took an interest and sent the short clip and photograph to our dear friend Shannon Phifer to ask her if she knew the horse. She simply sent back a photograph of Cavalier on the range, looking a million miles away from the shut down, scared wild horse now standing in the slaughter pipeline.

It was hard to reconcile the two images, and when I posted them side by side, it also shocked many of our followers, who immediately stepped up to help him get home. It was close to #givingtuesday, which is a unique day in Skydog's year when we offer to save as many as our followers donate to save. We add another save for every ten thousand dollars we raise, and every year, we seem to gallop past all goals for the number of horses we rescue.

We added Cavalier close to the end of the day's rescues, and his post exploded with people sharing it, and the people who love and follow South Steens horses on the range stepped up to save his life. It was a wonderful day in December when we brought Cavalier home, and

he stepped out of the trailer and back onto Oregon soil. He was home, albeit skinny and frail. We took it nice and slow and started by getting him some friends, Tesoro and Silver, and eventually, he was well enough to go out on land, decompress, and get away from pesky people.

This is where true psychological healing begins for wild horses: When they are back on huge acreage, with room to move and the ability to make choices for themselves, including where to go and who to make friends with. When we turned him out, he ran solo to the band of horses already out on this land and joined them without a squeal or stomp as if they knew he needed them. And among that small group of horses were two he knew well from the range, Commander and Rango.

OPPOSITE: *Cavalier*

I can't imagine how good it felt for Cavalier to see some friends from home and for them to tell him that the nightmare was over and that he could stop feeling anxious. He was home, and he knew it.

Along with them were some other boys who mostly, although not entirely, were rescued from kill pens like the one he had come out of. Henry and Wilson were two bay boys who had stood in different kill pens waiting and hoping to get on the right trailer, and thankfully, they got on ours. With kill pen horses, I often use the phrase, "It's inches and seconds," as that sums up the luck involved for these horses and whether a group or person steps up for them,

as to whether they land softly at a place like Skydog or back on to another trailer and into a situation that is less than ideal.

Wilson was a bay boy named in recognition of Scott Wilson, who has been to Skydog numerous times to take photographs of our rescued horses, which we sell to raise money for the animals in our care. Wilson was said to be blind in one eye, and Scott was particularly drawn to another killpen save, our pirate boy Jack Sparrow, so it was a perfect fit. Wilson loves cookies, and when you give him one, he smiles with all his teeth showing, and he has the sweetest personality out there.

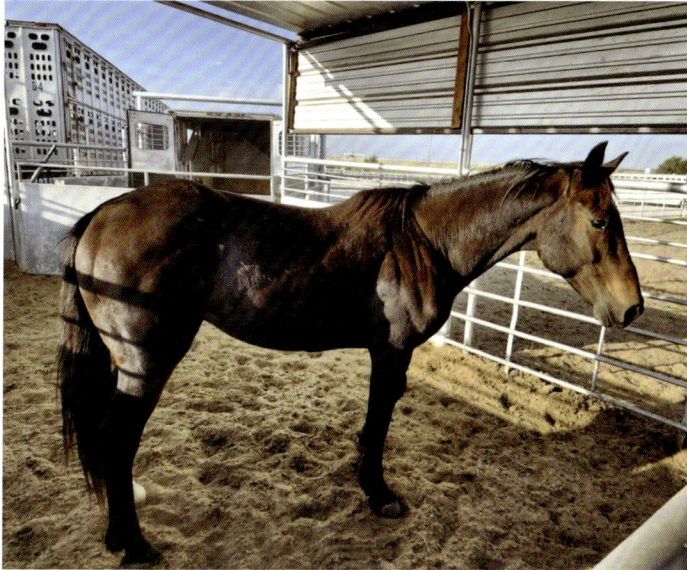
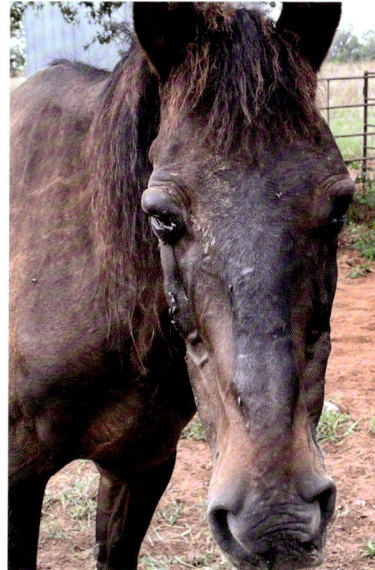
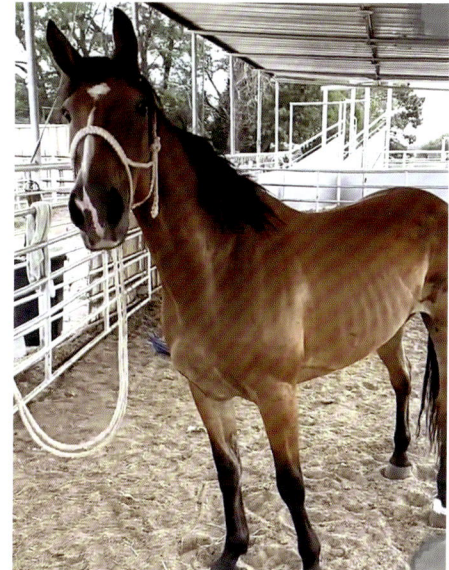

Henry was a Mustang we saw limping at a kill pen, unable to bear weight on his back leg due to a huge abscess, so we took this poor boy to provide him with much-needed vet and farrier care to help with his pain. He came to Malibu first and then on to Oregon when we realized no one had told him he was gelded, and he was acting like a horny Henry, and we needed to protect our mares from such naughtiness. He has joined Cavalier's group, with other South Steens royalty, and is another proud "kill pen save" joining over fifty such saves at our sanctuary.

One of the biggest reasons we take horses from the slaughter pipeline is to continually beat the drum for support for the Save America's Forgotten Equines (SAFE) Act, which is a piece of legislation that would entirely change things for horses in the USA. The bill would make it illegal to ship horses and donkeys across the border to Canada and Mexico to be killed for their meat and hides. It's a monstrous and inhumane death and one that should never be compared to humane euthanasia done by a vet. This piece of legislation is a bipartisan act that would be the holy grail for horses, wild and domestic, getting them out of this cycle of awful abuse and cruelty, which begins when they are taken to and sold at livestock auctions across the states. It's hard to believe that in this day and age, in what we consider to be a civilized society that is kind to animals, we would allow such horrific violence against sentient beings who don't deserve what happens once they are sold into the pipeline.

Two of the most prominent opponents to this legislation are, shockingly, vet associations and the Northwest Tribal Horse Coalition, representing five Native Nations in Oregon, Washington, and Idaho. Sadly, horses who live wild on reservations are regularly culled, and the mares and stallions are sent to slaughter for money, but as it's illegal to ship babies, they are taken away from their mothers and sold in large groups, usually into the slaughter pipeline, and often rescued by organizations who try to save them.

The two "big business" veterinary associations, the American Association of Equine Practitioners (AAEP) and the American Veterinary Medical Association (AVMA), have lobbied Congress in opposition to the SAFE Act under the pretense and myth that horse slaughter is "humane euthanasia" and that excess horses have nowhere else to go. Slaughter is the most inhumane process possible, from the slaughter pipeline—where weaker horses are bitten and kicked by stronger horses, many contracting various respiratory viruses and diseases that can prove fatal, especially to donkeys—to the transport, where the animals have no water or food for days, to the brutal way they are killed. It's monstrous.

This is why we fight so hard for the horses who land in kill pens and auctions, which are terrifying for unhandled wild horses. It's their last chance to get rescued, and we make sure to take a number every year no matter what else we are focused on. We know that telling the stories of these individual horses and letting people get to know and love these beautiful souls is the best advocacy we can do to stop this awful practice of horse slaughter once and for all.

To take action to get this legislation passed, go to www.skydogranch.org/oppose-slaughter.

OPPOSITE & ABOVE LEFT: *Cavalier* • ABOVE MIDDLE: *Henry* • ABOVE RIGHT: *Wilson*

Cavalier

This is Cavalier. He is a thirteen-year-old South Steens "Wild Horse" who landed in a kill pen in Texas. I had no idea if he was well known, but my good friend Shannon Phifer sent me a photo of him in the wild, and it's devastating to see what happens to these beautiful older boys once they're bought. Horses over eleven are sold "sale authority," which means the buyer owns them immediately and doesn't have to wait a year to get their paperwork. This so often means they end up in the slaughter pipeline straight away. This boy, who was so mighty on the range, was now reduced to an emaciated and terrified horse, confused and disoriented. Cavalier suffered the fate so many older horses do, and there has to be a solution to this broken system. Again and again, the BLM tells us they don't have enough staff to care for, process, adopt out, and check on these wild horses, but somehow, they manage to find enough people to keep rounding them up in massive numbers. This has to stop, as the protections granted them by Congress in 1971 have now been whittled away to be practically meaningless. Only the bald eagle and the wild horse have ever been granted protections by our government. Don't forget, it was President Richard Nixon who signed it into law. It's a bipartisan issue, and I don't care which side of the aisle brings in better protections for these horses as long as someone cares enough to do it. Meanwhile, Cavalier, you're coming home to a place where you will be respected and not called an "it" or a "thing," as you are in this video. Cavalier, you're coming to Skydog. ❤️

OPPOSITE & ABOVE: *Henry* • TOP: *Henry and Clare* • OVERLEAF: *Wilson*

"Wild horses merit man's protection as a matter of ecological right, as anyone knows who has ever stood awed at the indomitable spirit and sheer energy of Mustangs running free."

President Nixon,
on signing the
unanimously passed 1971
Wild and Free-Roaming
Horses and Burros Act

4

Family Reunited

THE STORY OF CRUISER, also known as the "luckiest boy at Skydog," came about thanks to a completely different horse and a story that, for the most part, had nothing to do with rescue. Our equine manager, Janelle, had always wanted to compete in the Teens and Oregon Mustangs training competition. Janelle has gentled so many wild horses for treatment or for handling when sick, and she wanted to try to gentle a wild horse to saddle and keep the horse to be her riding companion on the ranch, to ride fence on, or go look for a missing horse from a herd. She spent some time picking the right horse and settled on a boy who had been called Hidalgo on South Steens; she renamed him Ryder.

Janelle brought Ryder home from the BLM Burns Corral and started work on his gentling. Meanwhile, I received a message from a woman saying she had been at the corrals and seen a foal who had lost his eye and was worried he would be euthanized and would we consider taking him. Without thinking much about it, I sent it to Janelle with a photo of the foal with his mother. Janelle answered back, "That's Ryder's mother! And brother." What a crazy coincidence, and yet I know coincidences are God's way of staying anonymous and that this was meant to be. When the BLM came to do our inspection, I quietly asked Kayce from the corrals if it would be pos-

sible to adopt Ryder's mother and brother, and she said yes. The foal's eye injury made him unadoptable, and his mother, Jorja, was small and not particularly desirable to an adopter. I knew how much Janelle would appreciate knowing Ryder's mother was safe with us.

The next piece of the puzzle was the most extraordinary. Shannon Phifer, who helps the Steens horses come to us, told me she was in touch with a girl who had just adopted Cruiser, a well-known South Steens stallion, but she more than anything wanted him back with his mare, Jorja, and had no way to care for a wild horse, but wanted him to be safe. What happened

OPPOSITE: *Ryder*

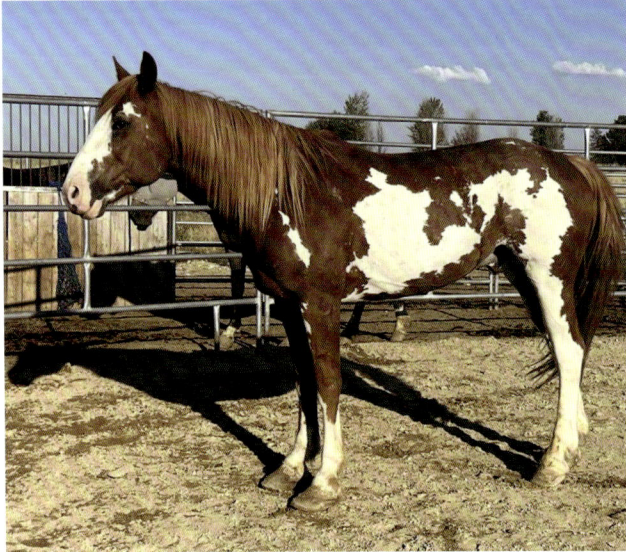

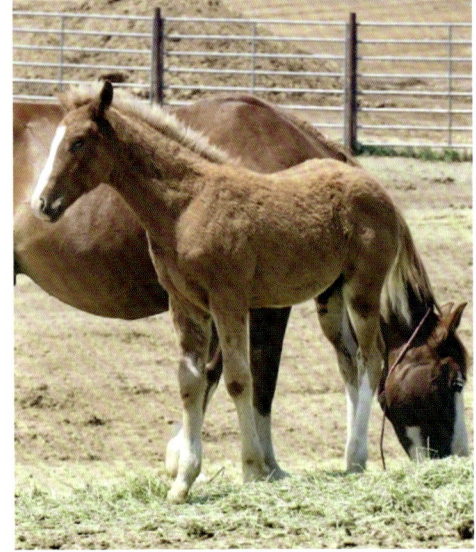

next became Skydog history: We arranged for Janelle to go pick up Cruiser, and we reunited him with his mare from the wild, whom he was besotted with, and his new son, Tupelo Honey.

It was a wonderful reunion, and tears were shed by all, including Shannon, who was there to photograph the event. The family ran around in the snow, happy to be back together, and I am not sure Cruiser could believe his eyes or his luck.

Over the next few months, as Tupelo Honey grew and had no issues at all with his lost eye, we started to add mares to the family to see how he and Jorja would tolerate additions. They all accepted them unconditionally, so we added Eden, a kill pen mare who had come in with our beloved Rooster before he passed away. We also added Honor, who had collapsed while being chased by a helicopter and had been roped and dragged into the trap during a roundup in Wyoming. We then adopted Nugget and baby JoJo to be a friend to Tupelo Honey, and they both loved having a playmate their own age. As it got closer to our turning them out on a 1,800-acre portion of the ranch, we added kill pen mares Pearl, Cinnamon, Nutmeg, and Onyx, as well as another mare we rescued named Wildflower.

With every new mare added, Cruiser became the most extraordinary band "stallion" (now gelding) and protector to all the mares he accumulated. Unlike in the wild, he didn't have to fight for any of them. Jorja seemed to think that the more friends she had, the better, and she bonded deeply with many of them, especially Honor and Nugget. We added Cedar and Cricket, special needs mares from the BLM corrals, and finally two kill pen mares, Rhiannon and Rose. All of them settled back into being wild horses and his herd is spectacular.

Old mare Eden became the most wonderful auntie to Tupelo Honey and Josephine and doted on them both, never letting them out of her sight when the entire herd was turned out on the huge area. Family was made at Skydog, and it was just as special as the other wild families. At the heart of it were Cruiser, Jorja, and Tupelo Honey, but these days, it's hard to tell who his lead mare is, as he likes to spend time with all of them—as does Jorja, who has so many mares to call friends now.

The saving of this one boy, Cruiser, via his son, Ryder, of South Steens, turned into one of the best families ever created at Skydog, and we could hardly leave this legacy out of this book, as they're two of the finest wild boys of Skydog.

TOP LEFT: *Cruiser* • TOP MIDDLE & OPPOSITE: *Ryder* • TOP RIGHT: *Tupelo Honey* • OVERLEAF: *Cruiser and band*

THIS SPREAD: *Cruiser* • OVERLEAF: *Tupelo Honey*

skydogsanctuary

Cruiser

Well, not only did Cruiser make it home to Oregon, but so did I. I wasn't going to miss a second of this magical fairytale for these horses. Janelle and Koal drove to get this special boy and carefully transported him home to us. He jumped out of the trailer and took off to the trees, he wasn't hanging around to say hello to anyone, and that's okay with us. Beautiful Jorja has no idea her love Cruiser is close by, and it will be the first time he sees their new son Tupelo Honey. I have goosebumps thinking about it. These reunions come along so rarely that we had to seize the chance when all the stars aligned to make this happen. Call it serendipity, kismet, coincidence—it's all of that and more. For us to be able to reunite a family is always special, but even more so this time, as they are all related to the horse Janelle chose for the trainer challenge. Another coincidence was that she took some video on South Steens and only recently looked back at it and realized it was Hidalgo, Jorja, and Cruiser all together, back when she didn't even know their names. When the universe speaks this loudly, we listen and take action, and it's an extraordinarily generous and selfless gesture for his adopter to want to reunite him with his family. She loved this family for years, and she loves Cruiser so much, she wanted his family back together. We know how much she'll miss him, and we are truly happy that she believes in wild horse family bonds as much as we do and would honor them. So Cruiser is home and thanks to the outpouring of love and generosity today, we won't have to worry about taking on another horse, so thank you. Not long now before we shall see them back together, and I, for one, am counting the hours.

5

Fighting for Freedom

A T THE START OF EVERY NEW YEAR, we have a board meeting where our board of directors decides what we will highlight and focus on that year. We decided that 2023 would be the year of the trainer returns and relinquishments: horses that were adopted to train for riding but who failed to transition to domestic life because they were just too wild. They also need sanctuary, so we were happy to adopt this theme for the year.

Our local BLM corrals contacted us when they heard about it and let us know that there were four candidates they would recommend for Skydog, so we headed over to check them out. In my opinion, there is no such thing as a bad-looking horse, but even so, the huge black horse we encountered when we met Metolius was an exceptionally beautiful animal. He was over sixteen hands and had the most incredible mane and tail and a bay-colored muzzle that gave him the appearance of a mystical creature worthy of starring in *Game of Thrones*.

When we spotted him in the corral, we noticed a little sorrel horse who went everywhere he went; they were inseparable, and you know how we feel about bonded horses. These two were quite clearly best buddies, and we couldn't separate them. So Coyote was given a spot, too.

Then we were shown another gorgeous wild horse from Stinkingwater, a dark buckskin whom we put on our list as well. There were a few other horses who had been returned, but we decided to let our followers decide how many we brought home with us by seeing how much we raised on the morning. We rarely do this, and usually only on #givingtuesday, but it was the start of the year, and we didn't want to use up too many sanctuary places if we didn't have the support we needed.

Coincidentally, I received an email from a young woman who had adopted a horse she loved and had sent him to a trainer, but sadly, when the horse turned out to be "too wild" to gentle, the trainer returned him to the corrals, deeming him too dangerous. His adopter was told he would be sent to long-term holding, but

OPPOSITE: *Coyote and Baby Blue*

she'd waited a long time and knew he was still at the corrals, and she asked us to take him. When I looked at her photos of him at the BLM, I recognized him as the dark buckskin we had been looking at. She had named him Rogue, and we decided to try our best to bring him, too.

On a snowy February morning, we headed to the BLM corrals in Burns, Oregon, and Kayce, who works there, had sorted some trainer relinquishments for us to choose from. We showed a video of the pen of horses and somehow people who follow the Onaqui herd in Utah recognized a horse they had known in the wild. It was such a crazy coincidence, and this bay roan boy was beautiful, but we probably wouldn't have taken him if we hadn't started getting deluged with messages asking us to help him. The people had spoken, and it was one of our most successful fundraising days ever, so we added Ariat to the group, loaded up, and headed home.

The girl who had adopted Rogue had asked if she could be at Skydog when he arrived, so she was waiting along with an amazing photographer friend of hers and ours, Shannon Phifer. When Janelle backed the trailer up to the gate, the whole thing was shaking because Metolius was so keen to get out, he was rocking it

and making a ton of noise. The explosion of that horse exiting the trailer was incredible, and he leaped out onto the snowy ground and took off up the hill with his little friend, Coyote. Then Rogue and Ariat leaped out and took off after them.

I will forever be grateful that Shannon could capture in her photographs the incredible moments of these four boys leaping out of the trailer and running around with new friends Pegasus and Rocky, who were already in the pen with Atsa. It was heaven to see them run for fun and for the joy of living. Metolius was such an imposing sight, with his long mane and forelock flying in the wind and against the white snow.

It always blows me away when I juxtapose the demeanor of these horses from when they stood at the corrals to their running through the trees and over the rocky ground with their newfound freedom. It's like they got into a time machine and came out the other end transformed into the wild horses they once were, with all traces of despair having left them. It will always be our privilege to give this to the horses who didn't take to domestic life and fought hard to keep their wildness. Giving them that one thing they clung to is the ultimate gift. Some horses are just meant to stay wild, and these four epitomize that want and need.

THIS SPREAD: *Metolius* • OVERLEAF: *Rogue*

Metolius

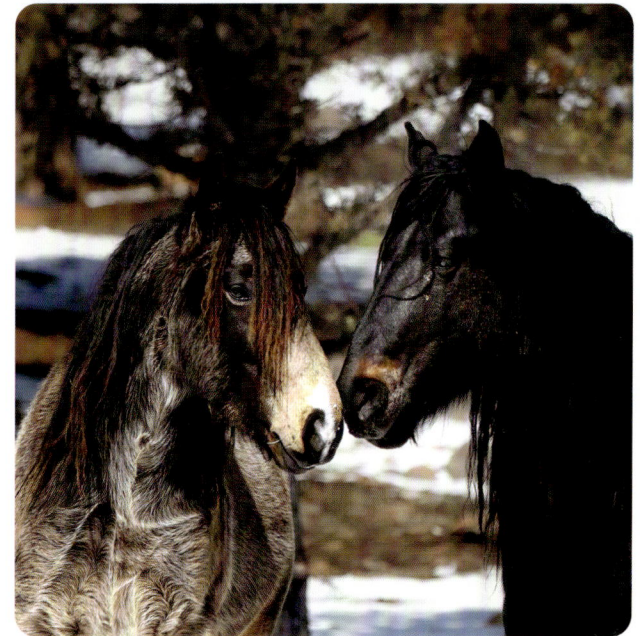

And I thought all the beefy wild boys were from Wyoming. Just check out the powerhouses Rogue and Metolius from Oregon. Wow, just wow. They are magnificent, and alongside them, our own boy Ariat from the Onaqui herd in Utah and little Coyote, who is from the same herd as our new Pony Boy from Shawave Mountains HMA in Nevada. But what they all have in common is that they went through a lot of training before being returned to the BLM corrals. They would have spent their lives in long term holding, doomed unadoptable, untrainable, and unsuited for domestic life. The giant U they get at the end of their brand number as sale authority might as well stand for all those things. But now it stands for useful and unique, unreal and unparalleled in their beauty and majesty. All of that and more. They take my breath away at how far they've come in accepting the people who care for them. Their emotional intelligence never ceases to amaze me; they understand intention and energy and react well. And so, they are our beloved friends, already jostling to say hello, be close, interact, and connect. They're special because, by holding onto their wildness, they made it here to get back to it, and I can't wait to see them head out in the spring to join the other boys. These boys have all left their huge footprints in our hearts, and every day they've been with us, they have my utter respect and admiration for being true to themselves. Just like Atsa, Pegasus, and Rocky. *The Too Wild Bunch*, forever.

LEFT: *Metolius* • PAGE 66: *Rogue* • PAGE 67: *Coyote* • PAGE 68: *Ariat and Rogue* • PAGE 69: *Ariat*

THE GOOD OL' BOYS

THE SENIORS HAVE MY HEART, plain and simple. And something about older boys being rescued and released touches me more than any other. A few old boys at Skydog deserve special mentions, and let's start with our two oldest: The Count of Monte Cristo and the king himself, Goliath. Both are extraordinary black horses but so different in look and demeanor.

Monte Cristo was, in fact, never meant to come to Skydog. We had made a donation to another wild horse sanctuary to take two horses we had rescued who were in quarantine and were victims of the BLM's adoption incentive program. We had rescued a whole bunch of them to get titles and proof that dozens of these horses were landing in the slaughter pipeline. When we brought them to us to vet them and saw how old Monte was and how few teeth he had, we knew that being out on just forage was not going to be suitable for him. We decided to keep Monte and then swap him out with a healthy and aggressive kill pen mare who definitely needed sanctuary and to be left alone.

So Monte stayed. He was a bag of bones when he first arrived, and it made me so sad that somebody had dumped such an old horse, completely unhandled and very wild, at a livestock auction, which led him to be in a kill pen in his late years. His name came from the herd he was from in Nevada, the Monte Cristo Wild Horse Territory (WIIT). It's a massive territory consisting of 71,680 acres of national forest land and 366,000 acres of BLM land, with elevations ranging from 6,000 to 11,000 feet. One of my favorite things to do is read about the different Herd Management Areas (HMA) these horses are from, as they teach us so much about public lands.

Monte is a wild, wild boy and never willingly comes near people. He lives with another of our wild boys, Sarge, in their own area near the main horse barn at Skydog Oregon.

One of the most interesting facts about Monte Cristo WHT/HMA is that curly horses are found within this territory and were introduced to this area by Tom Dixon in 1874. The most famous curly in the world resides at Skydog and was the horse who changed everything for

our sanctuary when we bid on him after he had been rounded up from Salt Wells Creek, Wyoming, in 2018.

Goliath is one of the only horses featured in this book whose story was told in our first book *Wild Horses of Skydog*, about the families at the sanctuary. Given his age and importance to us, we decided to include him again and showcase some of the most beautiful photographs taken of this old boy. His story is well known. About a year after I started Skydog Sanctuary, a few people I had previously worked with rescuing Mustangs out of kill pens contacted me and begged me to help the old boy. He was a well-known curly horse whom the BLM had captured during the Wyoming roundup. My friends had followed him and his family in the wild and were desperately worried about the fate of this twenty-six-year-old band stallion, who they all felt needed sanctuary and space.

I didn't know much about Goliath other than some photographs I had been sent. He was a massive boy who looked more like a bull than a horse, and it was with some trepidation that I said yes to bidding on him. We won the bid, and Goliath came home to us—and to an amazing surprise. We had also adopted his mare, Red Lady, after his adopter asked us to reunite them. It was an incredible moment seeing them reunite, and it confirmed what I had always felt: Family and the love these wild horses have for each other is real and palpable.

Goliath and his reunion with Red Lady was the save that changed so much for us as a sanctuary and brought us so many more followers, allowing us to save and rescue more Mustangs in need. He also convinced us of the value of family. As his and Red Lady's story was so popular, we went on to rescue dozens of other families, whom we featured in our first book.

Goliath is now the second oldest horse at Skydog at thirty-three; he is still going strong and is a magnificent example of a curly Mustang. We adore his curly coat, and I think he's the most magnificent curly Mustang ever seen. We are fortunate to have had so many photographers come to Skydog, and none of them leave without taking their own special shot of Goliath. He has been the most incredible ambassador for Wyoming Mustangs and the curly wild horses. They are beautiful and should be treasured and revered—not rounded up and wiped out.

Let's hope sanctuaries are not the only places to see curly Mustangs in the future, for being wild is where they began and should remain. Nothing is more beautiful than seeing one of these curlies in the wild, and we hope we will see them for many generations to come.

ABOVE: *Goliath*

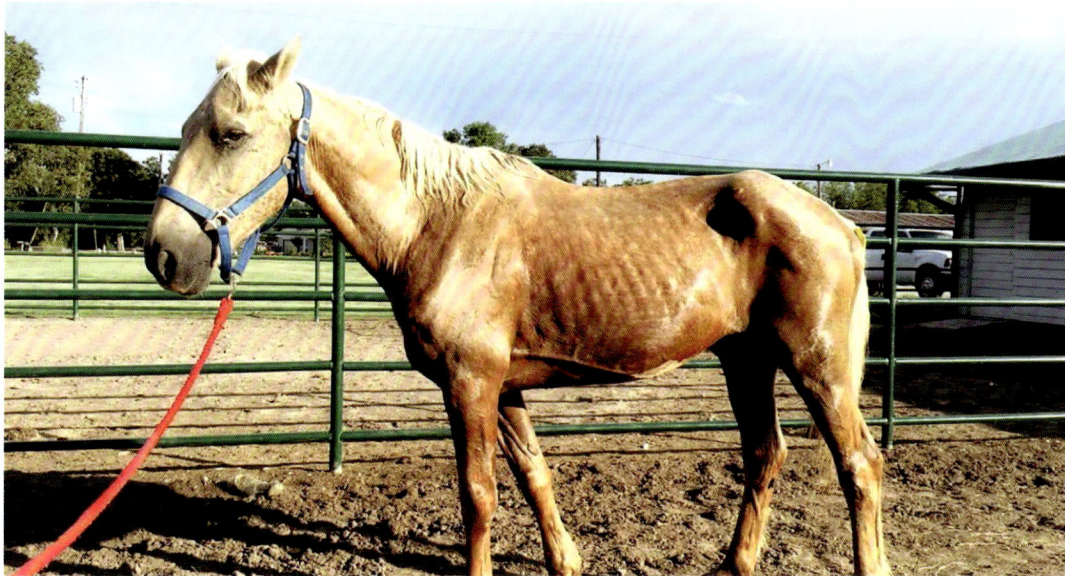

The last of the trio of oldest horses at Skydog actually lives with Monte, and his name is Sarge. This golden boy was an early save for us, and sadly, the first photographs of him starved at a kill pen are among the worst I have ever seen. He was so emaciated that it's painful to look at the before photos and not wince.

Sarge was saved from the kill pen by a rescue, then adopted out, only to be starved again. He was brought back, and we said yes to him coming to Skydog, as he was from Oregon, and we wanted to bring him home. We did it slowly in two trips because he was still very thin and needed to stop along the way for more re-feeding and rest. I will never forget when Sarge arrived: He was on a halter and walking nicely off the trailer, but when he got to his stall, he took off, dragging the person holding on to his lead rope with him. And that, we realized, is Sarge: a force of nature. He can communicate strongly to people—who I believe he thinks work for him—exactly what his wants and needs are.

Being contained with a halter and lead is unacceptable, and he will take off at a moment's notice if he doesn't like how things are going. He refuses to be blanketed and makes his feelings clear about what he will do if you try to coddle him. He also doesn't like having his feet done and will deliberately stand on your foot if you attempt anything he disapproves of. He is just a grumpy old man, and we love him. We will never stop taking the seniors, as there is nothing worse than seeing a horse who has given his all being abandoned when he needs people the most.

TOP LEFT: *Sarge* • TOP RIGHT & ABOVE: *Goliath*

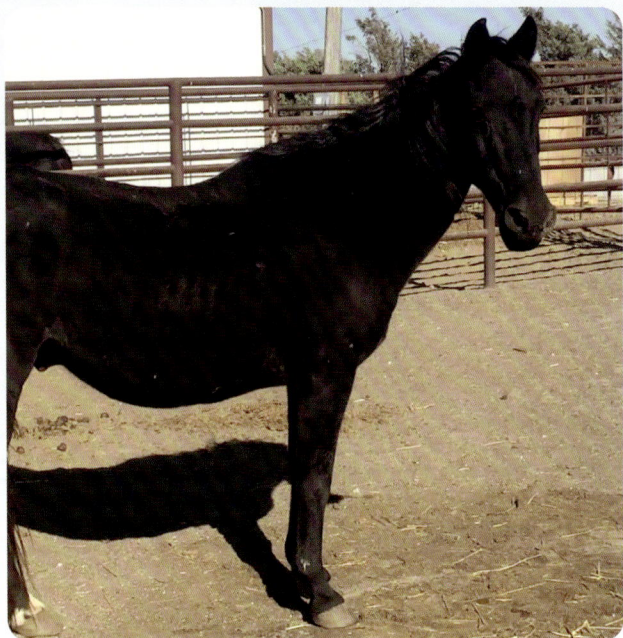

skydogsanctuary

Monte Cristo

❤️ 💬 ✈️ 🔖

Here is beautiful Monte arriving home to Skydog last night. This old boy was rounded up nearly thirty years ago in the Monte Cristo Wild Horse Territory in Nevada. To begin life as a wild horse and end it dumped in a kill pen at age thirty-two is a disgrace. This beautiful, skinny, uncared-for old boy deserves the very best of retirements and great care and comforts. He's like a velveteen bunny rabbit, and I can't wait to feed him and cover those jutting bones and deworm that swollen belly. He is such a gentleman and looks like he's wearing a black velvet smoking jacket and tuxedo. His eyes are so dark, they're like two shiny pieces of coal on his face. I want him to be with us for as long as it takes for him to understand and feel love and kindness, and I know he will grant us that wish. Part of me is glad old Monte turned out to have special needs, so we get to have the privilege of watching him come back to life. Thank you to all the amazing rescues we have worked with recently. We are all trying to show that working together helps the horses and each other, too. That unity and friendship are the way forward in this world of ours, and that there is no time for fighting when horses' lives are at stake. All of us working side-by-side to save wild horses—I couldn't be more proud.

RIGHT: *Monte Cristo* • PAGES 76–79: *Goliath* • PAGES 80–81: *Ember and Goliath* • PAGES 82–83: *Sarge*

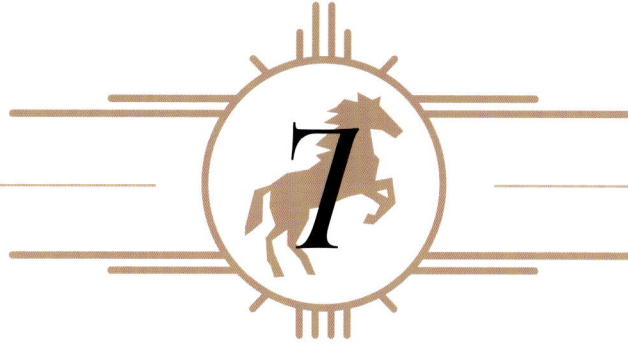

7

Senior Souls

LET'S STAY ON THE SUBJECT OF SENIOR HORSES and tell the story of a Mustang that is both extraordinary and extremely heartbreaking: the beautiful gray boy Lightning. When I first read the email about him, I was stunned and speechless that any horse could have survived what he did. The second I read his tale, I knew he had to come to Skydog so we could give him the retirement he deserved and so that he could finally know love and kindness. The only problem was that he was all the way in North Carolina, so we would have to raise a lot of money to bring him home. We told our followers about him, and there was the biggest outpouring of love and generosity. In fact, we raised more than we asked for, and those funds allowed us to pick up some kill pen horses in Kansas on the way home.

Lightning had been adopted as a colt and was from Conger Mountain, Utah. The man who got him didn't geld him and kept him in a small pipe stall and would occasionally throw a mare in with him to breed, but the rest of the time, he was restrained in this pen and pushed so hard against the bars that he bent them. His pen was never cleaned out, and the filth piled up so high that Lightning couldn't get under his shelter without bending down.

One night, his "owner" came home drunk and decided to climb on Lightning and ride him. The problem was he had never been ridden and threw the man off, badly injuring him, and he was taken to the hospital. When he got out, he went into his house, got a gun, and tried to shoot Lightning. Well, Lightning must have moved his head at the last moment because the bullet grazed across his forehead, leaving a scar to this day. Someone in that man's family asked a local rescue to come and get Lightning and save him, and he was taken to a rescue who then wrote to us to see if we could help him.

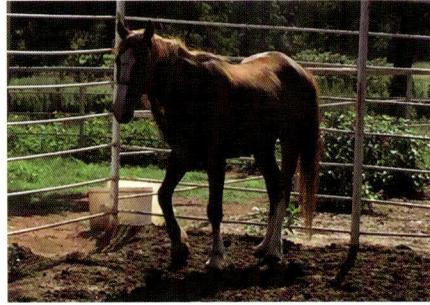

There was no hesitation, and he was picked up and brought all the way across the country—at the time, the farthest place we had ever rescued a horse from, but it was worth it to bring him home. As we had a mostly empty trailer coming west, we also picked up a couple of kill pen horses, and two of those were Gabriel and Leonidas—the latter named after a character in the film *300* played by Gerard Butler, who generously donated to the rescue.

Another older and very special horse we had to include is Read. He was the eighth horse saved by Skydog Sanctuary and remains one of our legends. Born in 1994 in Goshute, Nevada, I first saw a photograph of him in a kill pen in Oklahoma and visibly grimaced. His face had been horribly damaged by an in-grown halter that had been left on while he was growing and had eaten through his flesh and into his facial bones, completely exposing his nasal cavities to the air. In addition, he was incredibly wild, and I admit I was nervous about taking him.

He went to another sanctuary for quarantine, as we still hadn't closed escrow on Skydog Ranch, and we didn't want to bring him to Calabasas in a small space where we wouldn't be able to handle him. But he was in the second load to come to the Oregon sanctuary, and we turned him in to a nice-sized pen to get to know him. I named him Read after my husband, Chris, as he had done so much to help us start the sanctuary, including purchasing this 9,000-acre property with me.

TOP LEFT: *Lightning* • TOP MIDDLE LEFT: *Read* • TOP MIDDLE RIGHT, TOP RIGHT & ABOVE: *Donatello* • OPPOSITE: *Read*

Read settled down and, for a while, was alone until we added Swayze to his pen, and they became best buddies. It was good to see these two old boys, who had been through so much, now bonding and having each other to lean on. Read became the poster boy for our taking the very worst cases, medically, temperamentally, and physically. We soon had our hydraulic chute set up to be able to handle them for treatment of all kinds, and as time went on and we became more experienced at using it with our vet team, we took on even more difficult horses to help treat them and help them live out their lives sound and healthy. Read taught us so much, and now he lives with his mare, Blue, and plays bitey-face over the fence with Boomer to pass the time.

The third old guy is one we really don't hear a lot about but is a wonderful senior Mustang: Donatello. This boy ended up in a situation that animal control was involved in, as he lived in a place where dozens of horses were starved and neglected. His story is best told by Kelly, who reached out to us to find sanctuary for him.

"Donatello was born in 2002. He was captured and adopted, and the adopter put the Mustangs out into a pasture, and there was very little, if any, care given to the horses. They were allowed to breed, and soon, there were over twenty horses on site, and all were starving.

"Bluebonnet Equine Humane Society stepped in, and law enforcement seized the horses, and they were transported to foster homes. Donatello entered the rescue officially in 2011. He was rehabilitated, gelded, and sent to a trainer. And then another trainer . . . and then adopted and adopted again. You see, Donatello did not want to be a domesticated horse. He learned that he could buck off those annoying humans. Finally, the perfect adopter came along, and he went to his 'forever home.' Tragically, his new owner passed away, and he ended up back in a Bluebonnet Equine foster home.

"I was a foster home and inspector for Bluebonnet and regularly monitored the horses in the rescue. I noticed that Donatello was moved around a lot. At the time, I had started an equine-assisted mental health facility at my farm outside of Austin, Texas, and felt Donatello would be perfect to partner with our therapy teams to help humans heal from trauma.

"Donatello has a huge spirit. He was a wild horse, and that energy was always present. Earning his trust and building a relationship with him was an honor, and watching him teach humans how to be present and find their true selves was transformational for everyone involved. Donatello lived in a mixed herd for a while, but the mares in his pasture were not impressed with his constant need to gather them and move them around! I tried partnering him with a kind gelding, but Donatello felt he was a threat, and we had to separate them.

"So, Donatello lived alone in his own palace, with lots of hay and a run-in shed next to all of the other horses and interacted regularly with our therapy teams. But, one day, he started to gaze off into the distance. He started to pace restlessly and had a hard time settling down. I knew it was time to find a retirement home for this strong and brave Mustang.

"And so, I contacted Clare at Skydog Ranch in Oregon. There, the Mustangs live out their lives in freedom on 9,000 acres. I remember nervously waiting for the board to make a decision on whether or not he would be a candidate for the sanctuary. I literally jumped up and down with joy when I got the news that he was going to be joining this incredible place!!! Transportation was arranged, and off he went, our brave Mustang who had touched so many lives. Today, Donatello lives out his life with his herd, a wild one, running free, as it should be. It was an honor and privilege to have partnered with him. I will never forget him."

And here he remains until he passes away, like all the other wild boys in our care. It's our honor to have him as a Skydog resident.

THIS SPREAD: *Lightning* • OVERLEAF: *Donatello and Jasper*

Lightning

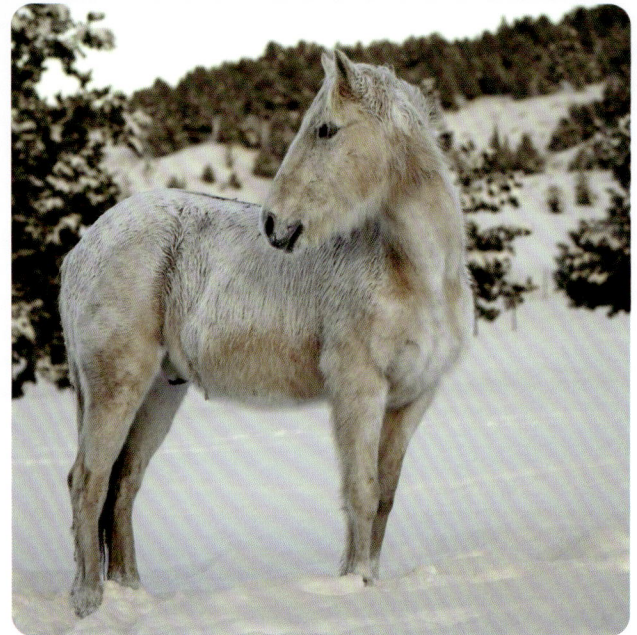

Gosh, it's so good to see this incredible boy having some fun and kicking up his heels. I wasn't sure he would ever mentally return from that dark place the circumstances of his life had taken him. But Mustangs are incredible, and they have the strength to live in the moment and move forward from trauma. This beautiful boy was confined for years in a tiny space as a stallion, and his story is one of the worst we have ever heard. But he survived, and look at him now—he has a huge space for him and his mares, as he doesn't like to share, having been gelded so late. He's making up for the lost years, the sad years, the bad years of his life, which he has put behind him. He gets so excited to see breakfast, and why not run and buck for the sheer joy of knowing another meal has arrived? He's put on weight, and he's calm and confident now. I hope he lives another decade or more so that these are the memories he will have when he finally lays his head to rest, having known the best of people and barely remembering the worst. White Lightning, you're a miracle, and thank you for sharing your joy and sweetness with us all this morning. You're a good boy.

8

The Three Amigos

WHEN WE RECEIVED A MESSAGE ABOUT THUNDER, little did we know that we were saying yes to such a wild and explosive horse. His story was a familiar one for the owner relinquishments we often agree to. The lady reaching out to us had taken on Thunder to get him away from the people who had him, as he had clearly expressed a desire to stay wild and not "be broken." It's gut-wrenching that the word *broke* is used to describe a horse who was once wild and then had their spirit broken, as that is exactly what they are referring to. It's an old cowboy term—and exactly how they saw the process. Thankfully, these days, a lot more people understand that the true gentling of a horse is a cooperative process that works way better in the long run for a good solid foundation for a horse to understand and enjoy.

A woman had rescued Thunder and then kept him in a confined space for years, as he was too wild to do much with. This kind and generous lady fed him, watered him, and mucked his pen, carefully moving around him—and aside from that, mostly left him alone. And we appreciate her doing that for him. We said yes and had our hauler go pick him up in California and bring him to Skydog Oregon. When she opened the trailer door, he burst out with so much energy and determination it was almost

frightening. We knew immediately he was unlike most other horses we had taken before him.

He actually had the rare distinction of being named "potentially dangerous" to go in with by Janelle, and I heeded her opinion each time I opened the arena door to feed and water him. He was a snorty dragon of a horse and seemed very defensive of his space and was full of fight or flight with not a lot of freeze. He was ready for anything, and it was sad to see him so scared and braced to fight for his freedom.

OPPOSITE: *Thunder*

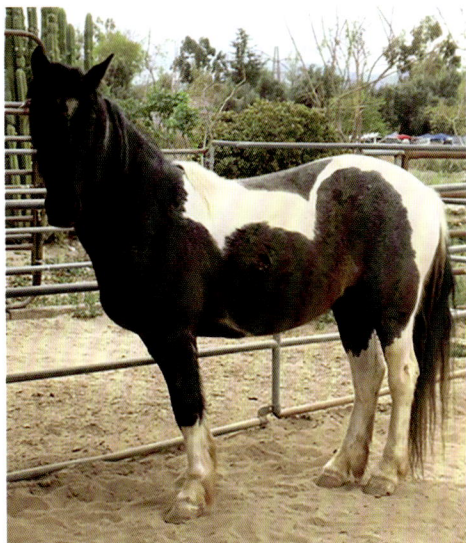

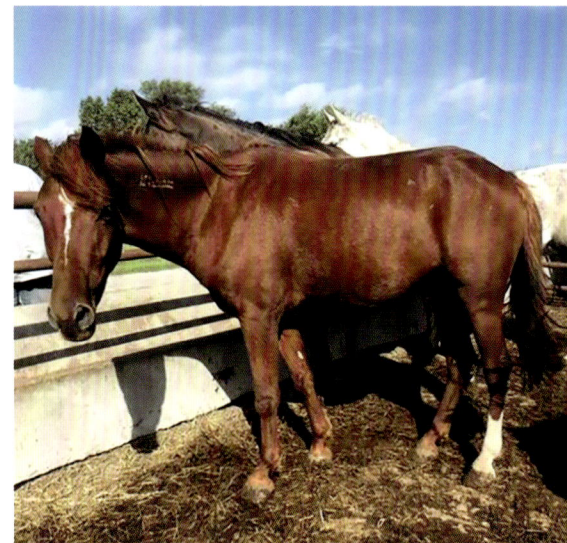

The best thing we could do to calm him down was to introduce him to a friend to see if he could be talked down off the ledge he seemed to be teetering on. We settled on Francis, a sorrel boy with a skinny blaze we had recently rescued from a kill pen in Texas. Francis was sold to the kill buyer by a man who had tricked a girl into selling the horse to him. He wanted Francis shipped immediately and not advertised, as he was worried the girl would see him and know he'd lied. Well, the one thing we can always depend on is for horse traders to be thieves and liars, so the kill buyer went back on his word and offered him to me.

We named him after Saint Francis, the patron saint of animals. It was on his saint's day that we saved him, and it seemed clear that Francis had an angel looking out for him to get him to safety and Skydog. By bringing this lucky boy in, we hoped Thunder could see through our interactions with Francis that the two-leggeds aren't all bad and that we meant him no harm.

It worked like a charm. Thunder calmed down enough to trust Francis, and we were much relieved that his new buddy had pacified the snorty dragon. They became inseparable, and it's hard to find one without the other no matter where they are today.

Then came the day when we turned them both out with the boys' herd, and that was a beautiful thing. Thunder had been confined for so long, and I think his biggest desire was to run again, have space and freedom, and get back to the business of being wild. And boy, did he run. He ran and ran for about two weeks straight anytime he felt like it, and the whole herd, with Francis at his side, came with him. They reveled in the joy he took in running, and, like all good herds, they wanted to stay together, so they went along for the ride. The number of videos I took and posted of the horses running the

entire thousand acres, from one side to the other, were admired and appreciated by all who had come to know and love Thunder.

Now with a new herd, Thunder took on another friend, who, up until then, had never truly bonded with a horse in his herd. That was River. River's story was awful and hard to tell. He was owned by a bad man who every night would get drunk and beat his horse. In my wildest dreams or nightmares, I cannot understand the psychology of someone who would have that much anger in them and take it out on something so innocent and kind.

In the end, the man's son put a halter on River and walked him several miles to a neighbor's house and asked the lady who lived there to take the horse, as he was worried his father was going to kill him. The heart and bravery of that little boy saved River's life. I know I'm not the only one who thinks about him, and I hope he's okay and knows River is safe. It breaks my heart what these horses go through, but I also can't help but think that anyone capable of treating a horse that way may well treat a child the same way. I hope and pray that's not the case.

So Thunder lives in a band of three now, with his two best buddies at his side, and he's happy. It has also been my great honor to be able to give Thunder cookies—if I can get him away from the other horses and catch his eye. We have an unspoken language he understands, and I stretch out my arm as far as possible, and he takes a cookie from me. And it never fails to put a smile on my face. Thunder is the original blue roan pinto who galloped into my heart long before Blue Zeus (who was one of the stars of my first book, *Wild Horses of Skydog*) was ever captured, but planted a seed that continued to grow when Blue Zeus came home and became the second blue roan pinto I adore.

ABOVE LEFT & OPPOSITE: *Thunder* • ABOVE MIDDLE: *River* • ABOVE RIGHT: *Francis*

skydogsanctuary · *Thunder*

Thunder, the sweetest wild boy in the West. It was cookie time for some of these guys, and it's always the greatest thrill when Thunder decides to come close. This spectacular blue roan pinto with a wary eye came flying out of the trailer when he arrived and didn't stop snorting for days. He was quite rightly defensive of people and had no real reason to trust them or want to make a connection. And I don't blame him—quite honestly, some people are vile and awful and horribly cruel. Many days, I prefer the company of these horses, especially after a rescue where I had to deal with such people. Sometimes, it feels like I need a good shower to clean my energy after having to interact with a kill buyer or even some at the BLM. The contempt they can show toward these horses is offensive for anyone. So, coming out for cookie time and being with such pure and decent souls is perfection. And just like that, I am surrounded by all that is good and honorable and honest. Thunder, River, Patron, Eastwood, Feather—these are great souls with enormous hearts for forgiveness and love. So I took an energy bath and walked away whole. 🧡

LEFT: *Thunder* • OVERLEAF: *River, Francis, and Thunder* • PAGES 100–101: *River*

*"You occasionally see one,
and it's the thrill of a lifetime.
But mostly all you ever see
is a cloud of dust after they
are gone. It's their stubborn
ability to survive that makes
them so remarkable."*

Velma "Wild Horse
Annie" Johnson

9

PARTY OF FOUR

ONE OF OUR FAVORITE THINGS is to go to the BLM corrals and look for special needs or senior horses to rescue and give them extra care and attention. We adopted two pairs of boys who made an incredible impression on all who got to know them, and both are still much loved and respected members of their herds to this day.

The BLM corral adoption staff contacted us about two injured horses at the facility. Chief hurt himself when he got hung up trying to jump the fence, so he was moved to a confinement pen, where he could heal in a smaller space, out of the crush of horses in the general population. Hawk had somehow been injured, and when the wound became infected, his fetlock had swollen to an enormous size and could no longer bear weight, so he was hobbling around on three legs.

We drove to the corrals to see them, and Wendy Rickman, who worked there and with whom I had always had a good relationship, took us around the back to see the two geldings. As we came around the corner, a wrangler on horseback opened the gate into the small enclosure they were in and scared Hawk so badly that he ran to get away and slipped on the ice and snow, falling

and going partially underneath the fencing. I held my breath as he scrambled back up on his three feet and stood in the corner shaking. I said I would take them, as this didn't seem like the best environment for healing for either of them. We did the paperwork and let them know we would come back once the snow was a little more melted so we could move them safely.

For me, a promise made is a promise kept, and so a week or two later, we were back with a trailer to take them home. One of the older wranglers was in charge of bringing them down to the loading area, and I quietly asked him not to push the horses hard, as one was injured, and to just go gently with them. I saw a look of contempt in his eyes that worried me, but he walked away whistling and swinging a rope. The next thing I heard was a crashing and a man yelling, "Ya ya ya," and

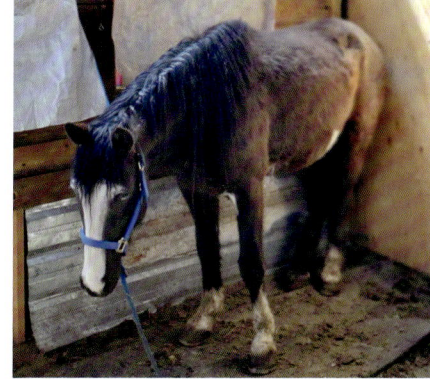

suddenly Hawk was barreling toward us in the chute at a gallop. As he got to us, he ran into the iron gate before him and smashed to the ground. I have to admit I thought he was dead, and I looked at Wendy, and that look said everything.

He stumbled back to his feet for the second time since I had met him, and I prayed he would make it out of there alive. I have never felt so helpless and sad for a horse in my life.

We drove home in semi-silence, and I was glad these two boys had each other and was comforted by that. We got them back, and the healing for Hawk began. He was a particularly wild and traumatized boy, but Janelle worked wonders with him, patiently and quietly winning his trust to be able to do X-rays and start the treatment needed to help him be comfortable and to wait until the bone inside his foot fused so that it wasn't as painful. The vet

certainly pondered euthanasia for him, but something in Hawk's eyes told us he wanted to fight for this new life he had before him.

At one point, we decided to remove Chief, as he was now healed, full of life, and running circles around Hawk, trying to get him to play and run with him. But one month turned into many as we marked several great milestones for Hawk in his progress and healing. Today, Hawk is out on rugged, rocky, mountainous land and has a family and friends and is well. You can still see the fused but weight-bearing place where the injury was, but he can run with the best of them and has the incredible wild life we weren't sure would ever be his again. Chief runs in another herd and has a palomino mare he loves named Bambi and a bunch of young colts he raised and taught to be Mustangs. They are both exactly where they're meant to be and happy as clams.

OPPOSITE & ABOVE LEFT: *Hawk* • TOP LEFT: *Hawk and Chief* • TOP MIDDLE: *Mesteño* • TOP RIGHT: *Rowdy* • ABOVE RIGHT: *Chief*

The other pair of boys we took from the Burns BLM came about after we suffered the two worst deaths we ever had during Skydog history. In one three-month period, we lost two of the greatest horses who ever lived and who will never be forgotten. Rain was a Mustang chosen for border patrol training who had failed the tests and was adopted by one of the trainers, who ultimately concluded that Rain would be happier in our sanctuary. We happily said yes to this stunning buttermilk-colored boy we had all fallen in love with at first sight.

Sadly, after a year with us, Rain had a complicated colic and was rushed to the hospital. We even did surgery with a 30 percent chance of survival because we just had to try to save him. But tragically, he didn't make it, and we lost him. It was a horrible loss for me, as I loved him a little too much and had spent so much time with him. Then Renegade, whose story I told in the last book and whose whole family still lives with us, passed away from a bad sand colic, which we couldn't save him from.

There was nothing more we could have done to save either of them, but somehow, we had to honor them and show what they meant to us. So we reached out to the corrals to find two horses to take their spots rather than heading to long-term holding, which is where they had been slated to go; they had even been hip-branded and were ready to leave. We wandered the pen full of boys who were about to disappear forever and tried to figure out which horses to take. Kayce, at the corrals, told us one of the boys had been adopted but returned and showed us a photo, and we knew instantly Rowdy, with one blue eye, would be the perfect way to honor Renegade, who had been just as unhappy in training as Rowdy looked in that photograph.

I let Janelle have the second choice, and she picked an incredible-looking dun who would not have looked out of place on the Kiger HMA with his dorsal stripe, long two-colored mane, forelock, and black mask. We named him Mesteño, as he looked like the foundation stallion famous for being the sire of so many Kigers to come. Mesteño was from Paisley Desert HMA, but he was joining the Skydog herd, and we headed home with them both. Our hearts were partially healed by saving two other deserving wild horses who needed their freedom back. They are still together in the boys' herd and spend the summers in Spring Valley, being as close to wild Mustangs as you can get.

OPPOSITE: *Hawk* • ABOVE: *Chief*

Hawk is one of the most extraordinary Mustangs I have had the honor of knowing. We were asked to take him by the Burns BLM corrals. He had been injured, and then infection had gotten into his bone, leaving him unable to walk or bear weight on his back leg, which was swollen and stiff. During the process of adopting and picking him up, I witnessed this beautiful horse run into panels three times, sending him to the ground. It was the most shocking and horrifying thing I have ever seen happen to a wild horse up close. And I can never forget that. So when I see him now, healed and enjoying simple pleasures, that image is also there in my mind, and the contrast is jarring. But this truly is the medicine that heals my heart of all the horrors these wild souls have endured. Roundups are not nonlethal solutions. They are horrifying and cruel, and to watch hundreds more Utah horses lose their freedom, and some their lives, this week is painful to all of us who love wild horses. I know it's sad to spoil this peaceful scene, but sadly, this is a rarity for Mustangs who are rounded up and put in holding pens. We can't save them all, but these horses and their stories can be ambassadors for all the others who don't have names but who matter and are just as special and worthy as this family. So, let's keep fighting, take action when asked, and keep being a voice for them wherever we can. We will keep raising awareness of the issues and showing people how incredible and special these wild horses are. Hawk, you are my hero. 🧡

RIGHT: *Chief* • OVERLEAF: *Chief and Georgie*

PREVIOUS SPREAD, LEFT: *Mesteño and Donatello* • PREVIOUS SPREAD, RIGHT: *Mesteño* • THIS SPREAD: *Rowdy*

10

THE MANE EVENT

It WAS A SPECIAL YEAR that landed these six horses at Skydog, each under different circumstances but ones that led them to unite as a herd, bonded by the trauma of roundup, neglect, and starvation. Ford was a horse that the US Forest Service asked us to consider taking. In the photograph they sent us, he looked like a dark-colored horse with a soft yet wild eye. They told us he had been adopted out but didn't adjust well to training, so he was returned by his "owner." They thought the best thing for him was a sanctuary placement, and we told them if they could wait until spring, we would take him.

At about the same time, a woman reached out about her horse, Tesoro. He had been her heart horse when they were both younger, but her parents had passed away, and she had to give him up and send him to a place she thought would be safe and where he would be cared for. Years later, she found out he was still there but now neglected, skinny, and in poor health. The woman fought hard to get him back and nursed him back to health with good nutrition and amazing care. Now, her life circumstances meant she couldn't keep him, and although she knew she could sell him for a lot of money for how he looked, she was desperately afraid he might end up back in a bad home.

So she reached out to us to take him and give him back his freedom, which she felt he still yearned for. She wanted him to run with a herd and get back to being a wild horse again. And we agreed. Something about her sincere desire to keep him safe, along with the faded photograph she sent of Tesoro in her email, nudged my heart to do this for both of them.

He traveled to us in the spring, just like Ford, and they began their journey at Skydog by each other's side—one wild, dark, and brooding, the other like a nugget of gold mined from the ground. His name, which means "treasure" in Spanish, suited him perfectly. They got along well, except when I came to visit Tesoro, Ford

OPPOSITE: *Ford*

would take off and watch in confusion at a distance while I untangled Tesoro's mane, which seemed determined to tangle itself back up regardless of how many times I brushed it out.

There is an old tale that the tangles in a horse's mane are knots made by the fairies to use as stirrups when they ride the horses at night while we're asleep. According to legend, it makes the fairies angry to undo these knots, so I always ask their permission and apologize to them while I'm working away on restoring Tesoro's mane to its long, glorious smoothness.

The next rescue was coordinated with Laura Leigh of Wild Horse Education, whose photographer, Marie Milliman, took photos and a video of a horse named Spartacus, who had jumped the trap sight after being captured in Nevada. He had leaped a high fence to regain his freedom, and apparently, this wasn't the first time he had evaded capture this way. He was a hero and a smart and determined wild horse.

Sadly, the video this time showed wranglers chasing him down on horseback, roping him to the ground, and leading him back into the trap he had escaped so many times before. Watching the video, I knew we had to give this boy back his freedom and preserve his wildness after all he'd been through. We were told his son Gatsby had also been captured in this roundup and was by his side constantly in the BLM holding pens in Litchfield.

We said yes, and Janelle and I traveled to pick Spartacus and Gatsby up and bring them home. It was a stressful loading, but we soon had them in our trailer and were on our way to Skydog Oregon.

The last two horses were boys we had met when we went to the corrals to pick up a horse we named Memphis. The staff had run Memphis in with a couple of other horses, and they were standing nervously in the chute, worried about being confined and their proximity to people. I took out my phone to video Memphis for social media, and somehow, I hadn't pressed record but had pressed to stop the recording and caught Dundee standing there when I took the phone out of my pocket.

I accidentally posted it to Patreon, thinking it was just a video of Memphis. People watched it until the end, where they caught a three-second glimpse of Dundee standing there. Well, there was no stopping them from repeatedly asking us to go back and get him. One woman even stepped up to sponsor and support him, so eventually, we were able to find the right time to go back and pick them both up.

Sometimes, it works to advocate for a wild horse and not give up, gently but firmly pleading the case. And it makes us so happy to be able to tell those people that their persistence paid off, and that's how Dundee and his buddy, Oliver, came to Skydog.

These six horses with six different stories started their new lives together with one another by their sides. Some were braver, some more fearful, but they all helped each other and ran out together into wild lands, where they found an area they called their own. It was an amazing experience to feed them every day and watch them get a little closer and less afraid each time I came to Oregon.

ABOVE LEFT, OPPOSITE & PAGE 120: *Ford* • ABOVE MIDDLE: *Tesoro* • ABOVE RIGHT: *Dundee* • PAGE 121: *Ford and Tesoro* • PAGE 122: *Tesoro and Spartacus* • PAGE 123–125: *Spartacus* • PAGES 126–127: *Gatsby* • PAGES 128–129: *Spartacus and Gatsby*

THE MANE EVENT | 125

skydogsanctuary

Dundee & Oliver

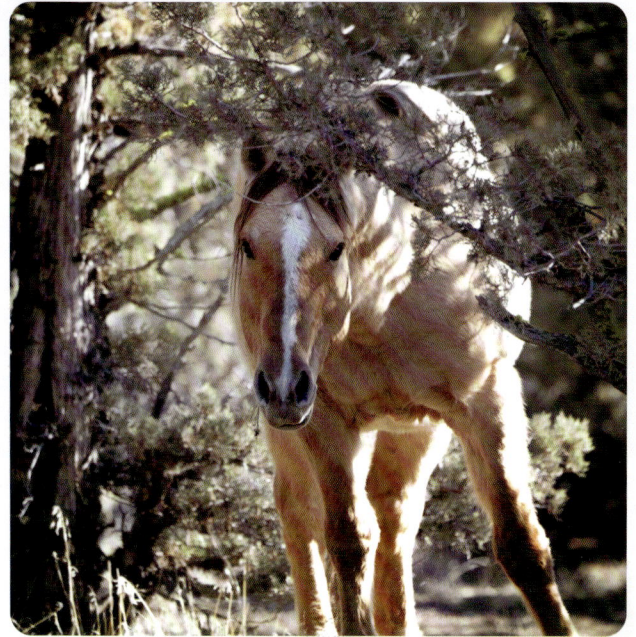

Seeing another two wild horses step out of a trailer onto Skydog soil is always a great reward for all the hard work we put into caring for the horses we have rescued. It's been an extraordinary day getting to know these two, and horses are always talking and telling you about them if you listen closely. That kick from Dundee as he was leaving said a lot. He wants to live life on his terms and nobody else's, and I'm so honored that we get to give him exactly that—choices and the freedom to be himself, kicks included. Isn't that what we all want, to live life on life's terms and be our authentic selves? Well, who are we to think we're the only ones? I hate the entire concept of humans having dominion over animals. Their obligation should be to care for animals and treat them with respect, and I guess here in this tiny corner of this wild world, that's what we're trying to do: to listen to them, honor their opinions, hear what they want, and give it to them the best we can.

Dundee and Oliver, it might have taken us a while, but the timing had to be right, and there were others who needed us more urgently. I think you all know by now that if we make a promise to a horse, we keep it; we were always going back. Thank you to every single person who donated, commented, shared, cheered us on, and kept us in your prayers. Right now, you are feeling the same sense of satisfaction and accomplishment that we feel for these two wild boys. We will let them settle, relax, and decompress, and then before you know it, they will be heading out to join Spartacus, Gatsby, and the rest of those wild boys. I think they're going to make some friends for life. And on we go again.

PREVIOUS SPREAD: *Dundee* • LEFT: *Spartacus and friends*

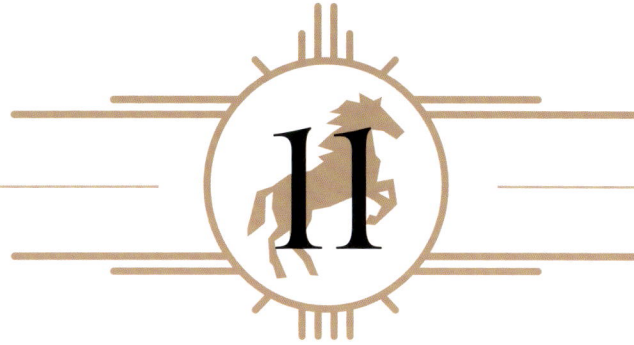

Family Is Everything

WHEN THE McCULLOUGH PEAKS HMA horses were slated to be rounded up, people who followed and loved them were beyond heartbroken. The herd is well known, as several photographers go out and take pictures of these horses, some of whom have been closely documented for years. We were asked to take two senior bonded pairs who had been together for a decade on the range: handsome gray San Jose with his mare, Black Beauty, and Las Vegas with his mare, Smoke.

Sadly, they were all bait-trapped by the BLM and taken to Rock Springs, Wyoming, where they waited for months to be adopted. The first batch to be put on the online adoption were the mares, and we, saying nothing at all about hoping to get them, quietly bid on them while all the attention was on the younger horses, including the daughter of Thor named Thora. That little filly ended up being the most expensive Mustang of all time and went for $60,000, which was extraordinary. There was a lot of insane and nasty backlash about her price, and everyone wanted to know who had adopted her. The adopters were so nervous that they asked us to take her and another highly bid-on mare named Moonshadow to keep them safe until the nonsense died down.

Our hauler traveled to Wyoming to pick all four mares up and bring them home to Oregon. Black Beauty and Smoke were clearly bonded, and it was also lovely to see how much they doted on little Thora and Moonshadow.

Next, the boys were put on the online adoption, but sadly, San Jose was left out due to the swelling he experienced after gelding, so we bid on Las Vegas. We reunited him with his mare, Smoke, and her best friend, Black Beauty, settled into the friend role while likely missing being with her long-time love, San Jose. Finally, in September, San Jose was put up for adoption, and we again bid without saying anything and managed to secure him for a low price. We have learned from years of bidding on online adoptions never to let anyone know who we

OPPOSITE: *Black Beauty, San Jose, and Smoke*

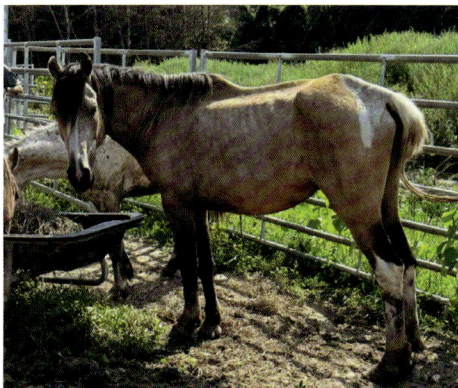

are bidding on due to nasty people bidding us up because they're jealous of our popularity or success.

Online adoptions bring out the worst on some Mustang sites, and their followers usually spend the entire week of the adoption bashing and writing nonsense about sanctuaries and rescues. It truly is one of the darker sides of the Mustang world that there are so many pro-BLM, pro-slaughter people who attack and hurl abuse online at any rescues or sanctuaries, and we have had our fair share of nonsense said about us. One of the most repeated fabrications is that we only adopt famous and flashy horses. Hopefully, they will all buy this book and see just how many unknown and unnamed horses fill our sanctuary.

San Jose had a bit of notoriety on the range, but we adopted him to keep him together with his bonded mare, Black Beauty, not because he was famous. We had our hauler, Steve Egner, pick up San Jose and bring him home, and there wasn't a dry eye in the house when he reunited with Black Beauty in one of our forty-acre pens. The only sadness we had is that Black Beauty and her best friend

Smoke were now separated, as we worried that the two dominant stallions (now geldings) would fight over the mares, as they had done in the wild.

While we let the four McCullough Peaks horses settle, decompress, and spend quiet time with their mares from the range, we were asked to be involved in a rescue that turned out to be quite horrific. A woman in Michigan had taken in thirty-nine horses, mostly Mustangs, from the BLM and kill pens, and twenty-six of them died of starvation on her property, leaving thirteen survivors, who had been seized by the county and were with a local trainer. These horses were so hungry they had eaten the carcasses of deceased horses close to them, and the whole thing was one of the worst hoarding and starvation cases I had ever seen or heard about. It made me shudder in horror at the nightmare these wild horses had been subjected to. We were asked to take a nine-year-old South Steens boy and the mare he was now bonded with, and we didn't hesitate to say yes. Sadly, he had been adopted to this place with a mare from South Steens, who had died of starvation there and

TOP LEFT & OPPOSITE: *San Jose* • TOP MIDDLE: *Hyas* • TOP RIGHT: *Las Vegas* • ABOVE: *The San Jose Six*

didn't make it. This is why in-person compliance checks by the BLM are so crucial and must be done.

Hyas had bonded to a young mare, Flower Moon, who had also survived, and they were inseparable at the trainer's place, where they were recovering. We said yes to both of them, of course, as respecting these horses' bonds and friendships is so important to us at Skydog. As usual, the wheels of justice turned slowly, and it took a while to get custody of the horses, but as soon as that was settled, a hauler brought them to Oregon.

Seeing them jump out of the trailer and run off onto land that would have been very familiar to Hyas was so special. They were home, and aside from the sadness of seeing their short tails (the horses had eaten each other's tails out of hunger), we felt good knowing those tails would grow back now that they were home safe forever.

We then decided to do something we hadn't done before: turn all six horses out together and see if they could make their own band without fighting over mares and get along peacefully. So, on a snowy winter's day, we opened the gates and set them free on close to a thousand acres of sage and juniper with its own stream and spring. On the first day, Las Vegas and San Jose got into a little fight for old times' sake, and I had some concerns. But by day two, Hyas and Flower Moon had joined them and seemed to have let them know that this was no place for fighting, and they had all settled down for good.

Seeing all six of these survivors together now in their own band is a beautiful thing, and the photographs of them together are all gorgeous. I am in awe of horses who have been through such hell and are now living their best lives in sanctuary. Their rescue and how they turned out is one of my favorite stories, and I love nothing more than to go out and sit and watch them live their days in peace and tranquility.

THIS SPREAD: *Las Vegas* • OVERLEAF: *Hyas*

skydogsanctuary

What a sight. 🧡 If this doesn't give you goosebumps, I'm not sure you're alive. 😊 We made a decision based on their personalities and dispositions to do something we rarely do and turn all six of these horses out together onto a thousand acres of beautiful land. We are careful not to always do this, as these boys can easily fight over their mares to keep and protect them. San Jose is a huge boy, and by the time a horse gets hurt in a fight, there is nothing we can do to help. These are wild horses with very strong, natural instincts, and the McCullough Peaks stallions are well known for fighting, so we discussed this for a long time, weighing up the risks and rewards. In the end, we decided as long as we could keep a close eye on them for several days, it would be the best outcome for all six, and the hope is that they settle, get along, and form their own band. That's not to say there won't be a little tussling in the short term while they figure out the hierarchy of the herd, but we have high hopes that this is going to be a wonderful outcome for all of them. So here they go, running back to freedom and taking back their wildness and destinies. And I can assure you there were plenty of tears on our end for this. Seeing San Jose and Las Vegas back in wide-open spaces, with hundreds of acres to roam with their mares, Black Beauty and Smoke, was very moving. Add to that Hyas and Flower Moon and all they've been through, with the horror they witnessed and experienced. It was no surprise they didn't have to think twice about heading out. So I hope this makes your day, too, and I will be posting lots of videos on Patreon and here as we follow their journey. Good luck and Godspeed to these wild horses as they move on with their lives and leave captivity in their dust. 🧡 This is Skydog magic at work. 🧡

LEFT: *Hyas* • OVERLEAF: *San Jose* • PAGE 146: *Las Vegas and Smoke* • PAGE 147: *Hyas and Flower Moon*

12

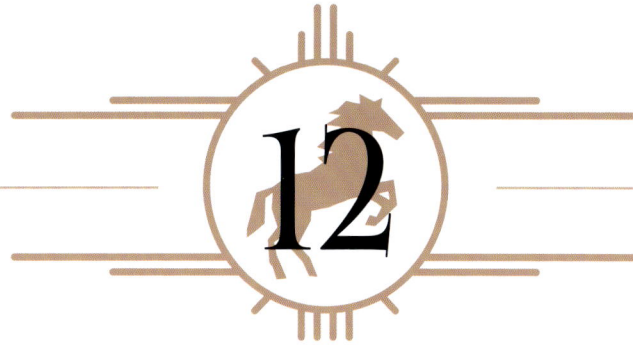

FLYING HORSES

Rocky and Pegasus are from Sand Wash Basin, Colorado, and were the first two horses we took from that area. We have very few horses at Skydog from Colorado, the first being Rain and the remaining mare being Colorado herself. We first saw Pegasus when a Facebook group posted a photograph of him flying over a BLM fence to get back to his herd, which was taken during the cataloging process for the online adoption.

Sand Wash Basin HMA has a ton of photographers who go out and take pictures of the well-known horses, and most of them have names and families who are well-followed. Usually, we don't look at the online adoption for these horses, as groups tend to get together and fundraise for them to go to local rescues and sanctuaries. Subsequently, they are less in danger and in need of soft landing than other herds who don't have Facebook pages advocating for them.

But the photograph of Pegasus, as they had named him, stood out because nobody knew this senior Mustang, and they deduced that he must be from outside the HMA and not used to humans, hence the terror that made him take that leap. They said he was incredibly wild and afraid, and he had quite clearly learned

that he could jump fencing to escape people and would most likely do the same in the future unless he went to those experienced in handling the wildest of the wild. Enter Skydog.

It was clear that we were the right group to take him, but we didn't want to take him alone, so we scoured the pages of senior boys for one who could travel with him. We wanted to find a horse with zero bids or interest, and in the end, there were two or three in that category. We made a last-second decision to bid on a silver bay Mustang whose intake photo showed him drenched in sweat with a wild and worried eye. We named him Rocky for the Rocky Mountains of Colorado, the state he was from.

Pegasus and Rocky traveled to Oregon and unloaded on a snowy day into a smaller pen, where they both took

OPPOSITE: *Rocky, Pegasus, and Atsa*

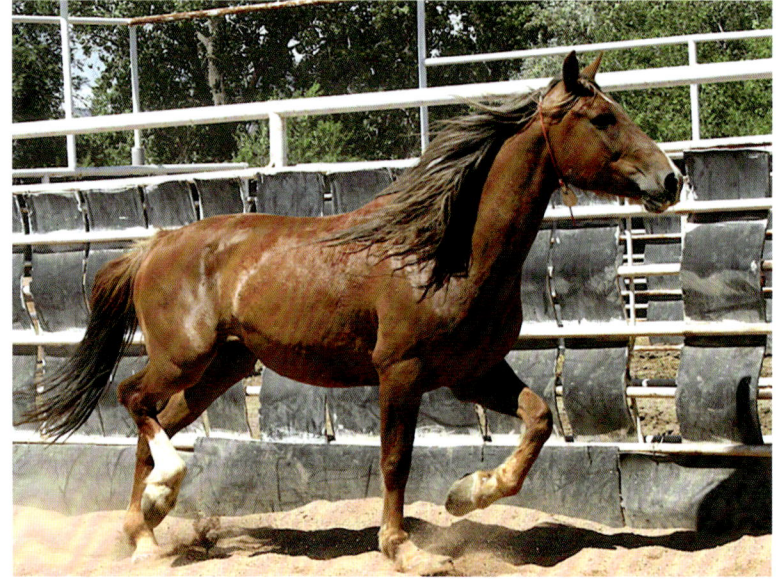

to hiding behind some skinny juniper trees. Pegasus, in particular, seemed to believe that if he couldn't see us, we couldn't see him, and he stayed away from us as much as he could. Once they settled in and got into a routine, we added Atsa and Gabriel to keep them company. It was a beautiful introduction, and meeting other senior Mustangs helped them relax and settle more quickly.

The day then came when we got back from the BLM Burns corrals with four new Mustangs in the back of our trailer. Shannon Phifer's photographs of Metolius, Coyote, Rogue, and Ariat running around with Atsa, Pegasus, and Rocky were incredible. The two boys from Colorado now had a herd, and they loved having friends and the company of other horses who had been through the same thing they had.

Being rounded up is horribly traumatic for older boys who spent their whole lives on the range, who had families and knowledge and wild instincts, which are way harder to overcome and dismiss when it comes to training and domestication. It is heartbreaking to see these once wild and magnificent animals reduced to mere shadows of their former selves. And nothing makes us happier than watching them return to their authentic selves. Truly, we wish they had never been taken from the wild, but for us to be able to give them back their freedom and remind them of their essence is a privilege and a blessing.

Extraordinarily, Pegasus joined two other older boys who had also made the leap to freedom when they were captured and penned. Phoenix, our first and the most known for it, had his photograph taken by Steve Paige, which was shared around the world and led to The Dodo doing a story about him, featuring his leap

and reunion with his mare, Ghost. Then Spartacus also learned how to jump the fence, and he did it more than once to escape. The visceral response of these wild horses to captivity is a symbolic and powerful feat that commands huge respect. That is how much they value their freedom and wildness, and it's sad that all three still lost theirs despite their heroic efforts.

We all value freedom, and nothing symbolizes freedom like the American wild horse. These animals would die for it, and sadly, some do. There are many instances of stallions breaking their necks, legs, and hips, smashing into an unfamiliar iron gate or pen, as they have no experience with the confines of captivity, given the endless freedom they grow up with on the open range.

Who are we to take that freedom away from them, especially at later ages when it's all they've ever known? The wisdom they bring with them, which ought to be cherished and passed on to new generations of wild horses, is lost with each horse who loses its independence. We must work harder to find solutions for these horses to stay wild and free. Millions of acres of public lands could be dedicated to wild horses if they were managed more effectively, with a more scientific and reasonable approach, considering carrying capacity and the needs of other wildlife.

With so many in this great country in support of having wild horses on our public lands, there must be a solution—we just need to find and implement it. Too many decades have gone by with roundups and holding facilities being the only tools in the BLM's toolbox. We need a new way of thinking about our wildlife, and we need to stop eliminating animals for financial reasons. Mother Nature has spiritual and intrinsic value that can never be measured.

ABOVE LEFT & OPPOSITE: *Pegasus* • ABOVE RIGHT: *Rocky*

skydogsanctuary

Pegasus & Rocky

From a photo sent to me a hundred times of a white horse leaping a six-foot fence at the BLM to this sight: Pegasus and Rocky arrived in Oregon this morning safe and sound and happy to jump out to freedom. To our crew: thank you. You're the best, and I truly mean that. You drove through the night, taking turns, resting every four hours, and keeping the horses hydrated, fed, and comfortable. These past couple of weeks have been painful, but moments like this make it all worthwhile and wonderful. Pegasus didn't even glance at the fencing to see if it was worth a try; with Rocky by his side, he was strong and self-assured. And Rocky—I don't have words for how glorious he is. How on earth did this magnificent boy have zero bids? It just goes to show there are diamonds in the rough: When you take what others have overlooked, you might just find treasure. I know others are celebrating their new wild ones today, and to all those new sanctuaries and rescues, welcome to this crazy wild-horse world. We are friends, not foes, and are always happy to help. But I'm sure you've got this, and your love for them will carry you through. So, while the crew gets some much-needed and well-earned rest, I just want to say thank you to all of you for supporting our work. One day at a time now, all is well—welcome home, boys. Welcome to Skydog. 🧡

LEFT: *Pegasus and Rocky* • OVERLEAF: *Rocky*

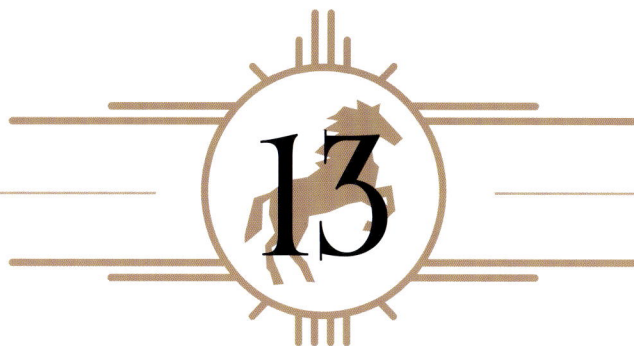

13

Dynamic Duo

PRESLEY AND SAINT WERE RESCUED from the same kill pen at different times, and their stories demonstrate the incredible differences in personality between Mustangs. They both were saved with a mare, but unlike other pairs who are rescued together and stay together, these pairs independently chose to take separate paths, showing that the transient bonds formed during the process of being rescued together don't always last.

Presley came as an addition to our rescue of Rising Sun, and both were named for Elvis—a singer I grew up listening to, whose movies I watched, and whom I named my first horse after. Rising Sun was the name of Elvis's horse, and she also looked so similar to Autumn, one of "The Ballerinas" (the name we gave to two graceful mares we featured in our first book, *Wild Horses of Skydog*), and was from the same herd. We saved her and then were asked to help a brown horse who was also in the Kansas kill pen, so we brought them together. Rising Sun was a sweet and pretty palomino pinto, and her partner was a brooding, handsome dun, a very wild boy who would take a cookie if you threw it on the ground but didn't want anything to do with people.

Saint was another horse in need at the Kansas kill pen. He was identified as an Onaqui Mustang, which is incredibly unusual to find in the slaughter pipeline, as they're desirable and their herd is well known. Again, we saved another horse to travel with him, and that was Miss Hedy Lamarr. As they came in around the same time as Presley and Rising Sun, they formed a foursome in a pen before being turned out with the big herd.

And then their paths took different directions by their own choice. It's one of the things I am most proud of at Skydog: choice. Once they get turned out, it's up to them where they go and who they make friends with. Once again autonomous and in charge of their own destinies, they choose the path that suits them and their wants and needs. In this case of these four kill pen horses, Rising Sun quickly decided she didn't want anyone to be

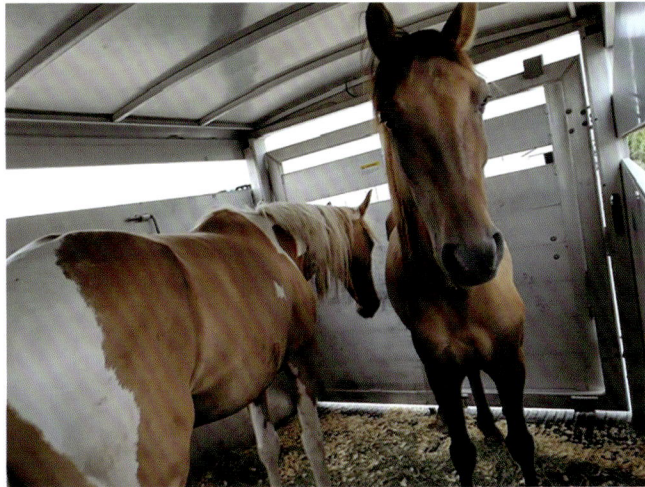
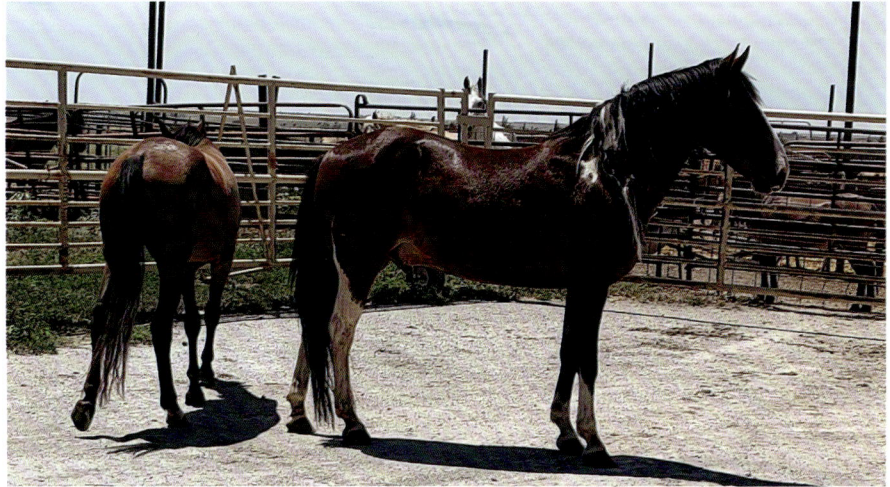
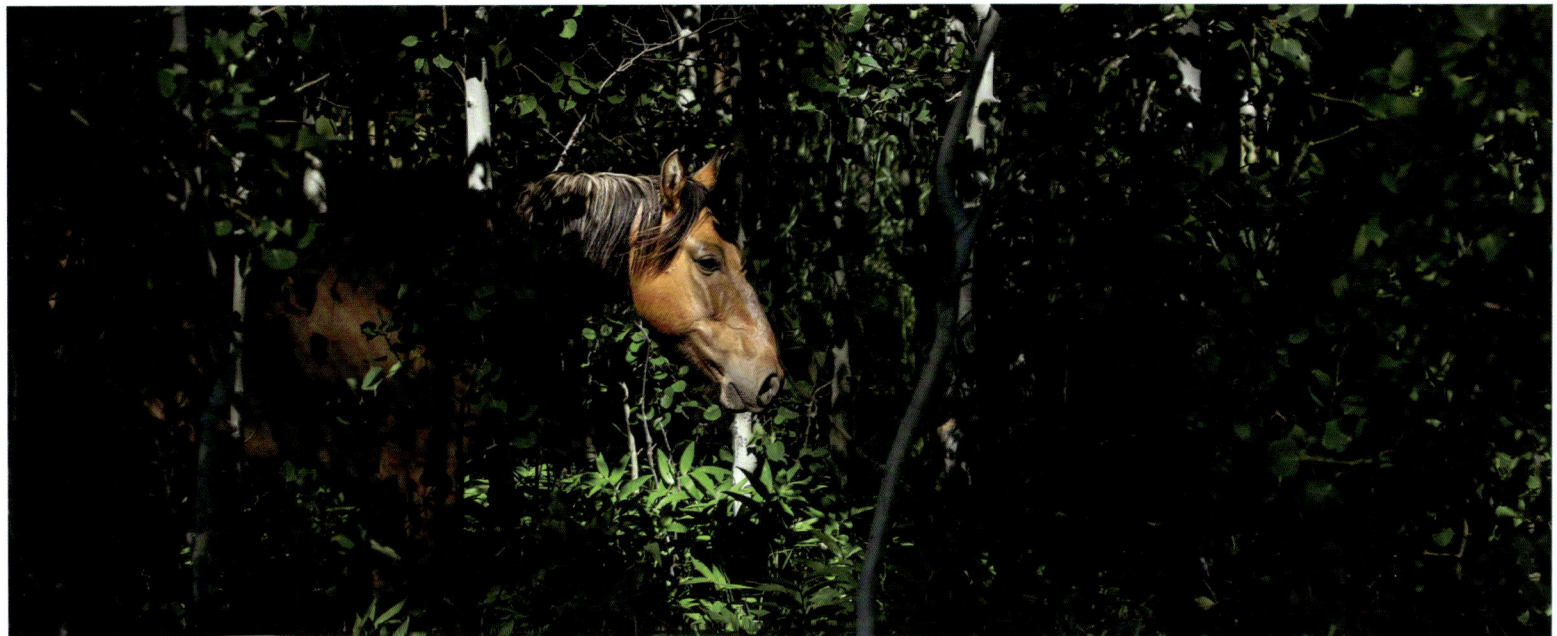

her boss and refused to be snaked and pushed around by Presley. Instead, she chose a group of girlfriends, including Lisa Marie, who she likes to eat with and spend her time around.

Presley, however, was determined to be a band stallion, as he might well have been in the wild before being captured, and he had his sights set on a family who had lost their patriarch, Renegade. Not only did Presley woo the mares Dahlia and Fern, but he also took on their sons, Outlaw and Rebel, as well as Aunt Paisley and Cookie, who had been standing in for Renegade since he passed away. Presley has become the leader of this incredible family—all except for Lupine, who decided to go on a hunt for a new love after her boy Renegade was gone.

Saint and Miss Hedy Lamarr also took diverging paths. Saint befriended Silver and his mares, who took on Lark and Hedy,

and they became a sweet sixsome with Silver in the lead. When Silver lost a lot of weight during the winter, he was brought in to be treated for a gastric infection, and kind boy Saint valiantly stepped up to take care of all five mares, keeping them together and safe for his friend Silver until he made it back out to the big herd in good weight.

Hedy Lamarr has wandered slightly and is often seen with Pete the Zorse. Time will tell if she joins his wild band and heads to Sheep's Rock in the spring. She is as wild as the wind with cookies on the side and has such an independent spirit that she may take some time to decide where and with whom she is happiest, and that is just fine with us. She is her own self and can make her own choices and decisions. We are happy to help restore these horses' psychological and physical freedom as they roam Skydog's vast lands.

OPPOSITE, TOP LEFT & ABOVE: *Presley* • TOP RIGHT & OVERLEAF: *Saint*

Sometimes, a wild horse stops and stares right at you. Through you almost. This new boy is flighty and suspicious, wary and worried. But for a moment, he stopped to ask a million questions. Are you kind, or will you hurt me? Can I trust you, or are you going to betray me too? Are you a friend or my enemy? Is this forever or just for a while? Why am I here? What is this place? Who are you? Is this home? So much was going through his frightened mind, trying to decide whether to stand or run again. But soon, the questions will stop, and the memories will fade. The trust will come and replace the fear. The anxious eye will soften, and his whole body will relax. Well, Presley, you sure did live up to your name, with your brooding dark shadows and ethereal beauty. These are Presley's numbers:

Tag number 16629915
Color—Buckskin (actually a dun)
HMA (NV0107) Antelope Valley
Capture Date: 09/21/2018
Sale Date: 09/03/2019

He's six years old, was rounded up at two, adopted at three, and who knows where he's been since September 2019. It's anyone's guess. But he ended up running wildly, blindly, terrified, and panicked at a kill pen in Kansas. Gentle boy, you are safe, secure, loved, cared for, and HOME forever. 🧡

LEFT: *Saint*

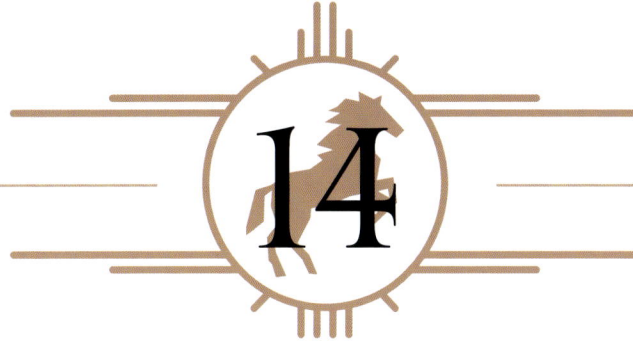

14

The One & Only

WE COULD NOT LEAVE BOOMER OUT of a book about wild boys. He is a Skydog original and fan favorite. His story wasn't particularly different or special to begin with. We were told he had been adopted from Virginia Range in Nevada and hadn't transitioned well to domestic life and was too wild to tame—a common story, but Boomer turned out to be a very uncommon horse. He came to Skydog, and we had him in the barn and wanted to find him a friend and tried him with both Maverick and OhBee, two older, gentle, and friendly boys who we thought might be a good fit.

If horses could speak, we would have heard them both yelling, "Get me outta here." Boomer had such a strange and odd way of interacting with other horses: no boundaries, way too clingy, and over-the-top possessive of them and their space. He would get right up in their business and then try to stop them from leaving by standing in front of them, blocking them with his body, and trying to keep them close to him. Neither of them appreciated it, and OhBee tried to be polite but, in the end, stood by the gate, asking to be let out and away from this strange horse.

We had never seen a horse behave like that, but we figured maybe it was just too small a space. We thought if we added him to a herd of experienced older boys, they would teach him how to behave and show him some manners. That isn't what happened. Strangely, he became dominant and aggressive with a herd, throwing kicks, running them off hay, and picking a fight with anyone who looked at him. We tried to give him a chance to settle, but he started guarding the water and not letting the other boys get to it and finally threw a kick at Kennedy, which fractured his leg.

Well, enough was enough, and we brought him in and put him in solitary confinement. He had also chased people carrying hay and run down a couple of dogs,

OPPOSITE: *Boomer*

skydogsanctuary

Boomer

This is Boomer's story, as told by his adopter: "I have a Mustang gelding named Boomerang who was removed from the wild for jumping into domestic corrals and breeding mares. He got the name Boomerang as they would drive him twenty miles out into the desert, and he would be back in the corrals before they got home. No matter how far they took him away, he would always end up back. So, he was captured. I saw a flyer for Boomer, a Virginia Range Mustang, and fell in love with him. Though I was a new horse owner, there was something about him, and I felt I had to get him and save him from potential slaughter. I sent him to the best Mustang trainers that I trust in our area, and they were able to do a lot with him. They let me know that he was a Mustang who had a very wild heart, so I chose to end saddle training as I didn't feel like it was what he wanted. We brought him home, and in that time, he went back and forth from being wild to allowing some handling. Two weeks ago, he stomped my foot, and I have permanent damage to it now. He didn't do it to be mean, but he spooked purposefully, something he does frequently. He spent two years in training, just trying to get him gentled enough to be touched. He also doesn't get along with any other horses. Sadly, I don't feel safe around him anymore, which is heartbreaking to me because I have poured so much into him. He is just a horse who wants to stay wild. I adore Boomer and do not give up easily, but after four years of doing my best, I would love for him to go to a sanctuary where he can run wild and be in a herd." Oh Boomer. ❤️

including Barkley, who was shocked, as no horse had ever been mean to him. I know reading all of this, it's hard to feel much love for Boomer, but we saw a horse who didn't know how to be a horse, and we heard reports about him being a loner on the range with no family or friends. He had taken to visiting a woman's ranch every day and standing at the fence trying to get in to breed her mares. Eventually, she called the BLM, and they came to get him—driving him miles away a couple of times, only to hear he was back at the ranch before they had even made it home.

He was captured and, sadly, had been separated again from other horses at the BLM because of his aggression issues. At this point, he was adopted by someone who asked us to take him after trying several trainers, none of whom managed to take the Boomer out of Boomer. We were now faced with a horse possibly spending his time alone again, but what happened next amazed us.

With a fence between him and the other horses, he settled into being the sweetest boy. He would play bitey-face over the fence with Read and flirt up a storm with Read's mare, Blue. He spent his day chasing the Polaris vehicles that went by on the road to get his exercise, and whenever horses went by, he put on such a show of running and bucking as if to say, "I'm Boomer, and I'm a star"— and he was. By now, our followers had fallen madly in love with Boomer and his antics. He was marching to the beat of his own drum and letting his freak flag fly as he went about his day.

Where once there had been brief discussions about possible euthanasia for his dangerous ways, there now was surprise and joy that somehow he had found his own way to be happy. He was fine living alone and seemed to have his own rich imaginary life where he was the star of every performance matinee. And he even came around to people. Boomer and I, well, we managed to make friends, too, and he would follow me along the fence line when I went for my evening walks. If I ran, he ran, and if I stopped, he stopped. It became such a sweet and loving relationship. When I get up to the ranch and climb out of my truck, Boomer nickers to me a gentle hello, which brings tears to my eyes and a smile to my face. I think he would follow me to the end of the earth.

He even accepted other people into his wild world. One time, we ran him up to the chute, and he was running around making a scene before going inside the barn. Suddenly, he ran up to Janelle and let her put a halter on and lead him in with no argument. He

THIS SPREAD: *Boomer*

was apparently tame after all, on his terms and in his good time. He slowly became more amenable to humans, and every morning, we would race up the fence line, where he would screech to a stop in the corner and wait for his cookie. Boomer had officially turned into a cookie monster extraordinaire and still chases me around for one.

About a year after Boomer had settled down, we went to rescue another horse we had been asked to take, as the woman who had her was getting older, and it was becoming increasingly difficult for the woman to get around. So Libby came to Skydog, and it was then that we found out that Libby had been one of the mares Boomer had visited at that ranch in the wild all that time ago. She settled into a pasture across from Boomer, and they somehow re-membered each other, and I would find them staring at each other.

After Libby had been here a while, we turned her out with Stargazer and Curly Girl to run wild with Blue Zeus's herd. It was all too much for Libby, who turned around and ran back to the pasture she had been in across the road from Boomer. One day, I just decided to give it a go. I was slightly worried about Libby's safety, but I let them out together in the space between their pastures outside my house, and they happily grazed beside each other, and Boomer behaved, well, like a gentleman.

We let them into a new pasture together, and there they settled into, if not domestic bliss, companionship, and they both seemed to do well. Boomer was polite; Libby never seemed to be entirely warm to the idea of him and was a little timid, but she stood up to him in a way nobody else had. She set boundaries and showed clearly what was acceptable and what was not. They lived together—more coexisting than a bonded pair—and several times, I caught them eyeing other horses over the fence. Libby had a crush on Tesoro, and Boomer was often caught down the hill playing kissy face with Lady Jade. They both had extremely good taste.

Come winter, Libby's arthritis in her hips was bothering her more, and we decided the best thing we could do for her was to move her to Malibu for the hot sun and a change of scene. She left and Boomer didn't so much as look up from his hay tub. It was for the best, and we have not given up hope that Boomer will meet another mare he loves in the future, and we will keep up the search for one. In the meantime, he's back to running the fence and chasing me around for a cookie. Oh, Boomer, you are unique, and we love you.

OPPOSITE & PAGE 171: *Boomer and friends* • ABOVE & PAGE 170: *Boomer and Clare*

15

THE GRAYS

E DON'T HAVE MANY GRAY HORSES, but the ones we do have are incredible. It's fascinating to watch their coats change color from when they arrive to how white they become. Gray horses are born close to looking black or dark gray, often with dapples, but by age eleven, they slowly fade and become almost entirely white in color, looking like completely different horses by that time.

The most striking example of the color change is with beautiful Koa. He is an Oregon Mustang rounded up from Three Fingers HMA. He left the BLM a confident and healthy young horse but later showed up at a Mustang competition as a shell of a horse, emaciated and terrified, to the point of making a top trainer cry. The organizer of the event took Koa home just to let him be a horse for two years, then sent him to a wonderful trainer to see if he could be retrained for adoption.

When the trainer started working with him, she realized how unfair it was to ask him to function like a normal horse after the abusive training he had been subjected to. The original trainer is no longer allowed to train for the BLM and has a history of producing very reactive horses—the same family of trainers ru-

ined and starved Charlie Eyebrows, leading him to be lame for a year when we took him. The woman asking us to take Koa told us he was a really sweet horse who is well mannered on the ground, but, as ones with sad histories tend to be, he is fine until he is not. He would have meltdowns at random times with ever-changing triggers when learning new things, and he was a hazard under saddle, even if he went without a panic attack for months.

When he came to us, he had muscle atrophy not befitting his age, a stiff gait, a hind end imbalance, and failed a brief neurologic exam. We wondered if he would fare well going back to being a wild boy on rugged ground and running the hills, but of course, he shocked us all with his transformation after he could move around in

OPPOSITE: *Koa*

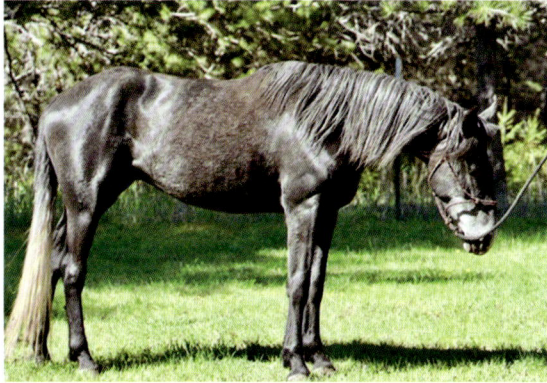
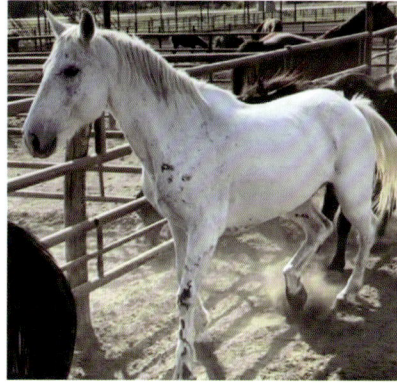
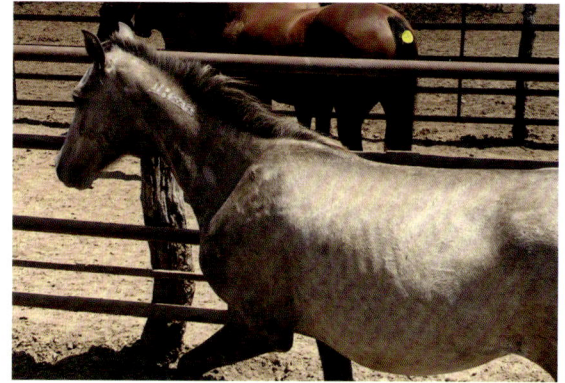

our wide-open spaces. He also became best friends with Bowie when he arrived; they are never far apart.

Bowie is another gray who came to us with the most perfect set of dapples, a wild personality, and a story not dissimilar to Koa's. Maybe their experience bonded them, as they both had undergone traumatizing training. I have nothing against wild horses being trained, but there are some pretty brutal, cruel, and unnecessarily aggressive trainers out there. You have to be so careful whom you choose, as bad or too-fast training can ruin a wild horse for life. Quite literally, it can blow their mind. Bowie's adopter said it best in the letter she sent us advocating for sanctuary placement: "I am inquiring about a space for a very special BLM Adobe Town gelding. He was failed by his first adopter/trainer, whom he attacked twice. He was more than just wild; he was terrified and completely

unable to relax in captive life. I offered to take him to rehab him and figured the least I could do was give him peace with us.

"But he is still not a happy horse. Some days he is okay, but other days he is reactive, terrified, and unreachable. I can handle him, but it's not enjoyable for him at all. I have no goals for him except his relaxation and happiness. His heart is enormous, and he has never hurt me; even in the middle of panicking, he will do anything to avoid harming me. He doesn't kick or bite and is the sweetest soul trapped in a life not right for his spirit.

"I don't have the ability to give him land and a herd here, and my heart aches to deny him what makes him flourish and thrive. This precious boy deserves happiness. I have tears in my eyes writing this. His welfare is all we care about, but to see him thrive as he once did in his homeland would be a dream for us."

TOP LEFT, ABOVE & OPPOSITE: *Koa* • TOP MIDDLE: *Milo* • TOP RIGHT: *Scout*

Of course, we said yes, and he's running the hills of Skydog, as free as he loves to be.

Another gray who joined the Skydog herd more recently was Milo. He was a kill pen horse rounded up from New Mexico, a state we had never rescued a horse from before. He was from Bordo Atravesado and was born in 2010. His story tells the very sad tale of a recent development in horse rescue. He was actually fundraised a few months earlier by a "rescue," who then horribly betrayed the horses by shutting down their page and dumping them all back in the slaughter pipeline.

Milo had a bonded mare he was rescued with who was lost, sadly. Milo was completely terrified at the kill pen, confused and shaking, and we had to help. We also found placement for the group of Mustangs dumped with him and worked with other organizations to get them the softest landings. Milo turned out to be the snortiest boy and still likes to give a dramatic blow and stand tall when he sees a person. Then, he remembers people can be good and comes over for as many cookies as I have in my pocket.

The last gray I wanted to focus on is little Scout, as his story is an interesting one—his rescue set into motion a campaign by Skydog, which ultimately proved successful. When the BLM introduced the Adoption Incentive Program (AIP) in 2019, we deeply feared the cash offer that would come with every adopted wild horse and burro. Although it was designed to help cover costs like training, veterinary care, or facility improvements, we knew that it would bring out the worst people, quick to make a dollar off wild horses before funneling them into the slaughter pipeline to their deaths.

When we saved Scout and his friend Angel from a kill pen in Kansas, little did we know that this pair would be the very first horses, just over a year past the introduction of the AIP program, to be adopted for the money they came with and then dumped at auction. Both were unhandled and very young, and it was hard to believe that our worst fears were now becoming a reality. Over the following year, we saved hundreds of wild horses in large groups out of kill pens and worked hard to place them with other rescues and trainers, setting them up for success and a good life after what they had been through.

THIS SPREAD: *Bowie* • OVERLEAF: *Bowie and Koa*

I spoke at the Wild Horse and Burro Advisory Board meetings, sounding the alarm to BLM management that this program was leading to the slaughter of so many animals, more than any rescue community could keep up with. We attended a virtual workshop with the BLM to see if we could suggest alternatives to the program that would keep the horses safer and not send them straight into the pipeline, with no handling, worming, training, or hoof care—just a sea of wild horses we desperately worked hard to network and rescue. We then initiated a lawsuit, along with American Wild Horse Conservation, to force the BLM to stop the program, using the evidence we had gathered, including the title and story of our boy Scout, the heroic little guy who started the whole campaign.

In February 2025, the judgment came down in our favor, and the Adoption Incentive Program was overturned and immediately suspended. Judge Martinez's order represented a landmark victory for wild horse protection, and in particular, the judge's statement that it was "not hard to imagine" that the slaughter of wild horses could be "fairly traceable" to the BLM's actions regarding the national AIP program and its failure to meet legal requirements for vigorous public comment and agency review.

The ruling found that the AIP program incentivizes "the unnecessary suffering and slaughter" of federally protected wild horses and burros, which was incredible. Our little boy Scout sounded the alarm and provided evidence that this program was doing terrible harm to wild horses and burros, and, for now, the program has been paused. Long may it remain that way.

The other grays in the Skydog herd are Slash, Silver, San Jose, and Swayze, who we lost last year in Malibu. They are some of our most loved and easily recognizable horses, who we can always spot way up on the side of a hill no matter how far away they are.

THIS SPREAD: *Bowie* • PAGE 182: *Scout* • PAGE 183: *Milo* • PAGES 184–185: *Scout*

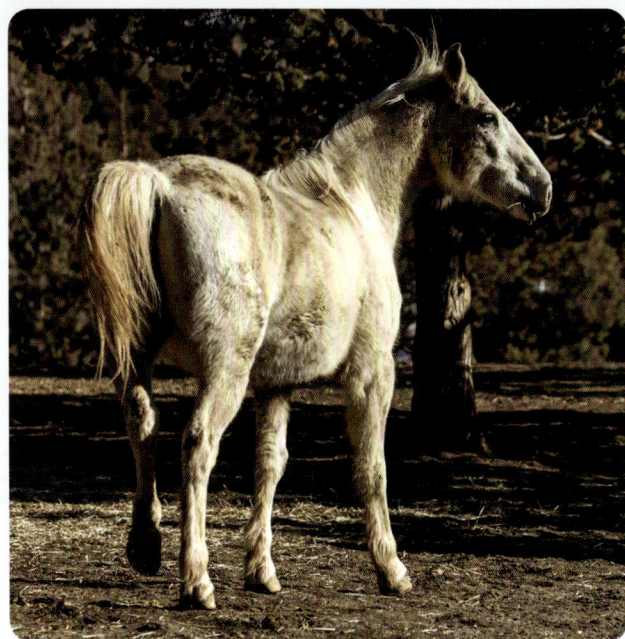

skydogsanctuary   *Milo*

And San Jose wasn't the only white horse we saved this year, as we took in this boy Milo on #givingtuesday after he had been betrayed twice and landed in the slaughter pipeline, the second time after the rescue who took him in dumped him and others. It seems like 2024 was also the year of the bad horse rescue; with so many springing up for all the wrong reasons and horses suffering at their hands, it has become a social media circus. So many horses and donkeys have died after being "saved" by people who had no business, knowledge, or experience, raising their hand to take free horses fundraised for by others who should have known better. The ongoing mess and mayhem caused by these characters continue, with horses being used as hostages to make these people money off their suffering. Truly, this year, I've seen some of the most despicable characters, who call themselves "rescuers" and thrive on the drama of social media fame and infamy, perpetuate the suffering and nightmare of horses and donkeys who had the misfortune to land in their greedy, grasping hands. So, we do what we can to educate and warn people against donating to mass bailers who care not one bit about where the majority of horses they rescue end up. Thankfully, we worked with a wonderful equine rescue to take the group Milo was in, and they have two of the beautiful fillies, who are doing well and loving life now that they have landed softly and safely. Milo is an older horse, but boy, does he think he's a naughty, wild dragon horse who loves to put on a show. We have one more white horse, Casper, who I will feature this weekend and who's in Malibu. The year of the black-and-white horses has saved some deserving and much-loved souls—thank you for supporting rescue done right.

RIGHT: *Milo*

16

Lucky Tales

THESE FOUR BOYS are all deserving of a place in this book, as each of them highlights a different aspect of Mustang rescue and the places where these horses can end up. Butler was the twenty-fourth horse we saved as Skydog Sanctuary back in October 2016, shortly after we received our approval to become a 501(c)(3) nonprofit. He was run through the Eugene Livestock Auction in Oregon, and all we knew about him was that he had been used as a pack horse in the mountains. He was an extraordinary color, a chocolate palomino, and has been a favorite to catch the lens of many photographers who have visited Skydog.

We paid a couple hundred dollars for Butler and picked him up at the auction the morning after we bought him. He was such a gentle soul, but you could tell he wanted to be as far away from people as possible, so we started to make a small herd from some of the other boys we had rescued at that point. We were heading into our first winter and wanted to do that with a small group while we learned more about the horses we had saved and the land they now called home.

Shortly after saving Butler, we pulled Kennedy from a kill pen in Sunnyside, Washington. He was a sorrel Mustang born in 1997 on South Steens, with a white blaze and striking blue eyes. When he got to us, we realized he was horribly sick from strangles, which is a highly contagious and infectious disease that affects the upper respiratory tract of horses, causing fever, nasal discharge, swollen lymph nodes in the head and neck, abscesses in the lymph nodes, difficulty breathing, and a cough. Bend Equine made countless trips out to the ranch to treat him and lance the horrible abscesses in his neck. Kennedy was sick for close to two months, which is an extraordinarily long time to have this disease.

He was isolated in the Elk Barn, and I would see his blue eyes peering through the gaps in the wooden

OPPOSITE: *Butler*

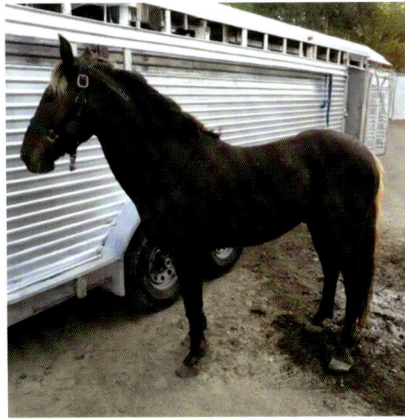

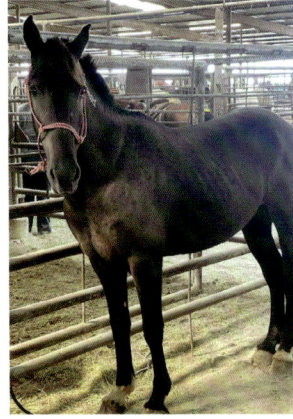

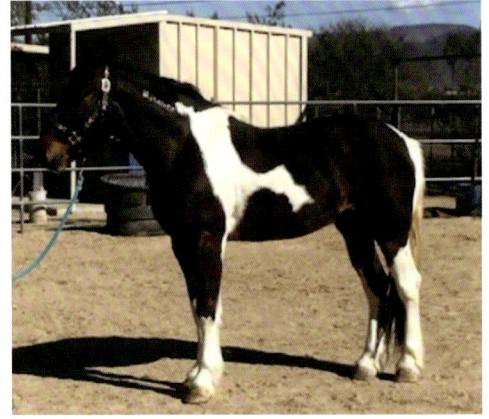

fencing as he watched people go by and horses in the distance. I would shout, "Not long now, Kennedy," as I drove by, hoping he knew this isolation would soon be over. The pictures of him from during this time are heartbreaking. We take biosecurity very seriously and take extreme measures to prevent the spread of the diseases these horses can catch while in the slaughter pipeline. These days, we tend to quarantine off-site to ensure nothing comes to the ranch and keep our current population safe.

Finally, Kennedy was allowed to join other horses, and the one he buddied up with in the small group was Butler. They have never been apart since. Kennedy is now twenty-eight but still strong, living with the boys' herd and doing great. It's always good to see this pair, and it shows how deep the first bonds made at Skydog are.

Apache was an owner relinquishment who thankfully never set foot in the slaughter pipeline, but sadly, his story is one of confinement and frustration. He'd been rounded up as a yearling from Fifteenmile HMA in Wyoming. He was adopted out and spent the next eleven years in a ten-by-ten-foot pipe corral. During that time, he wasn't trained, and any human contact was negative, leaving him traumatized and terrified, mostly of equipment. He was then with an experienced trainer for four months,

TOP LEFT & OPPOSITE: *Butler* • TOP MIDDLE LEFT & ABOVE: *Kennedy* • TOP MIDDLE RIGHT: *Gris* • TOP RIGHT: *Apache*

who told us he had only ever seen one other horse as reactive and dangerous as Apache in his twenty years of training horses. After trying to transition Apache into domestic life, they knew what he needed most is space, freedom, and wildness.

Apache, a beautiful bay pinto, is a stunning boy, and on the ground, he's a sweet and gentle horse who wouldn't hurt a fly. He was in Malibu for a winter with Cisco before going to Oregon. He now runs with the boys' herd and spends summers in Spring Valley, where the living is easy, and the wide-open pastures go on forever—a peaceful life for a once wild and free horse to retire into.

The last boy to introduce here is sweet Gris. He was spotted at the Bowie auction in Texas, and we decided to help him, as he was from the Red Rock HMA in Nevada, and a woman who knew him well in the wild asked us to help him. He also came to Malibu first and eventually traveled up to Oregon with Maestro's son Bo so that he could return to being a wild boy. We managed to catch Gris at auction before he ended up in a kill pen, but he was just as deserving.

Gris, Kennedy, Apache, and Butler are all the most amazing souls you could meet, and we are so glad they are all exactly where they need to be. We hope that by telling their stories, we can raise awareness and reveal the many elements of the rescue world: the places where the horses end up and the terrible diseases they encounter in the slaughter pipeline, having to interact with all kinds of sick and injured horses they meet. The slaughter pipeline is a filthy place, and no horse should ever have to go there.

We also hope beyond hope that this will be the time the Safeguard America's Forgotten Equines (SAFE) Act—legislation that would stop the transport of equines over our borders to be killed for their meat and hides—finally gets passed, and this pipeline to death for these horses and donkeys ends. I wish we could save them all, and it's my greatest sorrow that we can't save more. But all the horses with us are ambassadors, raising awareness and educating people about the horrors; then, we can all step up and do what we can. I am so grateful to our incredible followers for supporting our work and the sanctuary with the high costs we carry to keep these animals safe, cared for, and protected forever.

ABOVE: *Apache* • OPPOSITE: *Gris*

skydogsanctuary

Butler

♥ ○ ◁   ⊏

Just a horse on a hill . . . Here is another of the mountain beauties giving us all the feels. This is Butler, named for Gerard Butler, who helped us rescue him. And he is certainly as ruggedly handsome as the man himself. Butler was found in a livestock auction, and all we knew about him was that he had been used as a packing horse in the mountains. So here he is back on another mountain—except wild and free with nothing on his back. He is a chocolate palomino and looks like a Rocky Mountain Horse with his ombré mane. He is twenty-two years old and from Coyote Lake in Oregon, so he is right at home here and has blossomed being left alone, as he isn't a fan of being handled. So enjoy his posing and great angles and stunning natural beauty—Butler, you're incredible. 🧡🤎

OPPOSITE & PAGE 196: *Kennedy* • PAGE 197: *Gris* •
PAGES 198–199: *Apache*

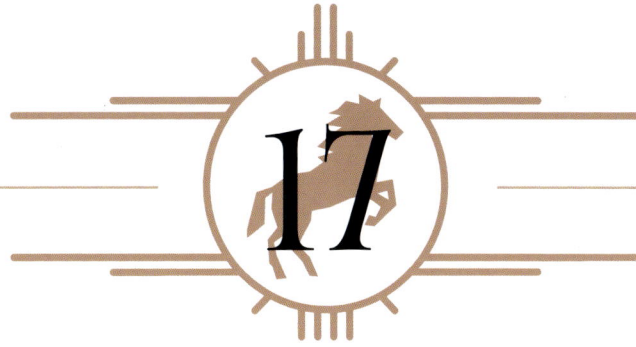

17

THE GOLDENS

Let's spend a chapter with some of our golden boys of Skydog. Firstly, beautiful Driggs, who was born in 2006 in Saylor Creek, Idaho. We'd considered bidding on him on the online adoption, but he received a bid, so we hoped he was going to a good home. We saw him again when his adopter wrote to us about the possibility of giving him back his freedom, as he wasn't settling into domestic life. He also had a lot of scar tissue on his front knees, which sometimes caused him pain.

Initially, he had been coming along in his gentling, but when he went to a TIP (Trainer Incentive Program) trainer, he regressed to being fearful of people again. This is such a common complaint and issue: Horses do well, slowly and gently, with their adopter, but when they are sent to a trainer to get "under saddle" for riding, they backslide, becoming reactive and fearful from too fast or aggressive training. Mustangs are not cookie-cutter, one-size-fits-all training candidates. They are unique and individual and need to be known and understood to help them feel confident to move forward and trust the humans training them.

Driggs's family, who loved him, could tell he was unhappy being domesticated and needed to be free again. At the time, we were very committed to taking owner relinquishments and horses who clearly demonstrated a desire to be free and away from people. It's much harder for older Mustangs to adjust well to training, having spent most of their adult lives wild and free, but we stepped away from bidding on him on the online adoption to give him a chance to do that. And we were happy to step up when his loving adopters realized he wasn't a good candidate for training.

Next, we have gorgeous Bobcat. I saw some photographs of him at a kill pen in Texas, and he was a sixteen-hand palomino Mustang who was said to be "bomb proof" and could be ridden by an "old lady." It came at a time when I missed having a riding horse and was thinking nostalgically about being able to ride the trails in summer and, at the same time, rescue a horse from the slaughter pipeline. I paid for Bobcat's bail and

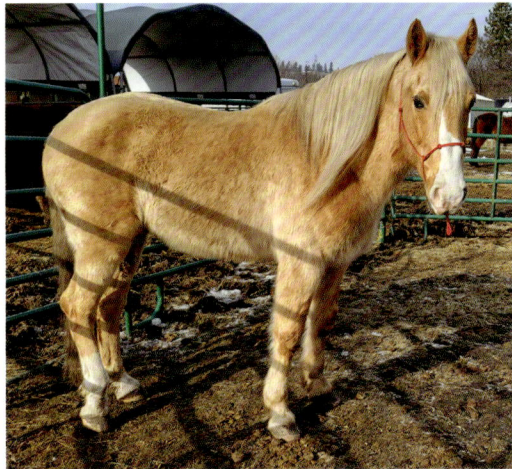

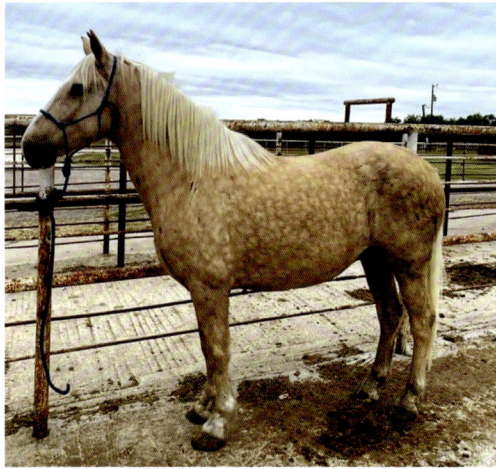

haul and feed myself, hoping he would be my new riding horse, another golden boy to replace Buddy, who was now retired and living out with his beloved herd.

I brought him to Malibu to see if he liked the idea of being ridden, and before I could find out, I got an email from the woman who'd had Bobcat for most of his life. Incredibly, this was the first time in our history that anyone had reached out about a kill pen horse we saved, telling us the history before the rescue.

She told me his name was Dirty because he had black swirls on him. She had loved him, but he would always buck her off if she asked him to trot or run. She had sold him a few times, but they always brought him back for the same reason.

She had no idea that one of those people had taken him to auction instead of bringing him back and that he had ended up in

a kill pen. She thanked me profusely for saving him and told me not to ride him, and that was that. He was moved to Oregon and officially became a rescued Mustang, and my dreams of reviving my riding pastime became just that. My memories can suffice, as I had such a wonderful life riding horses I loved. Now, my relationship with them is different but still just as beautiful—on the ground as opposed to on their backs.

The third golden boy is Champ, and he came about as part of our rescue of Goliath, our glorious black curly boy who did so much for our sanctuary. Goliath was rescued on an online adoption, along with two other Salt Wells Creek HMA boys, Maestro and Champ. Another organization called the CANA Foundation bid on and won them, and I had promised not to bid on them, as they wanted them. I was super happy they found a great spot and sanctuary.

TOP LEFT & ABOVE: *Driggs* • TOP MIDDLE & OPPOSITE: *Bobcat* • TOP RIGHT & OVERLEAF: *Champ*

skydogsanctuary

Bobcat Choice

Here, at our ranch in Malibu, is beautiful Bobcat, who I have just noticed has two swirls between his eyes. A swirl is a patch of hair growing in a different direction—also called whorls, cowlicks, and trichoglyphs—found on the horse's forehead, flanks, and numerous other places. A horse's swirls are formed before birth and never change. The forehead swirls are considered to be the most indicative of temperament because the forehead hair is the first to grow on the embryonic fetus. It is thought that the development of swirls is linked directly to the development of the brain. So what does it mean when a horse has two whorls next to each other? The size and placement of the whorls are all important, and apparently, multiple swirls on the forehead can indicate multiple personalities. High and tight side-by-side swirls, like the ones Bobcat has, can mean a horse who is super focused and talented but challenging and difficult in the wrong hands. So now I know. 🤎❤️ This beautiful big boy was rescued from a kill pen in Texas at the end of last year, and I think most of you know I am madly in love with him. He's such a special boy and gives the best hugs. Most of the horses at our Oregon sanctuary are wild, and so we don't interact with them in the same way, but here in Malibu, we have some older, special needs and gentle horses who most definitely love being handled and hugged. Bobcat, I didn't need to read your swirls to know you're special and talented, and I couldn't adore you more if I tried. ❤️

They contacted us a couple of months later and asked if we could take them after all. Maestro was "big medicine," which meant he was super wild, built like a bull, and didn't like being confined. Knowing him now, I absolutely agree this was the right place for him. I knew nothing about the third horse other than a photo I had seen of him in the wild with a beautiful family. But they both traveled to Oregon together, and the story of Champ began.

We had a photograph of Champ and his family in the wild, and, with that bedraggled picture in hand, went on the public tour at Bruneau in Idaho, a BLM off-range facility where the Salt Wells Creek mares had been taken. We turned up with a long-focus lens camera and a determination to look for any of the mares Champ had had on the range and bring one home for him. We saw a lot of grays and palominos that day, but none had markings that matched Champ's mares. We looked and looked but sadly found none of his family that day.

With a heavy heart, we had to accept that Champ's family was lost, so we did the next best thing: We built a family for him with a bunch of mares we rescued one by one. Little by little, he got his freedom back and a new family of mares. They are devoted to him, and he runs a tight ship. The mares include Daisy, a horse rescued from the Palomino Valley BLM after she was returned for being untrainable; Gypsy Rose, who had ended up in a kill pen after winning a Mustang training event; Kat, an owner relinquishment who had also "failed" her training and wanted to remain wild; and the three mares from Buddy's small herd in Nevada, who had found themselves lost in an off-range pasture for years until we brought them to Skydog.

And so, Champ came back to life and health and left his trauma from the roundup behind him, and now leads his band of merry mares around their own few hundred acres, where they often all take off, tails and heads high in a cloud of dust, when they see us coming. Champ is the third of our golden boys who call Skydog home, and we are proud to be their caretakers, defenders, and protectors.

OPPOSITE: *Bobcat* • ABOVE: *Champ and mares* • OVERLEAF: *Champ*

18

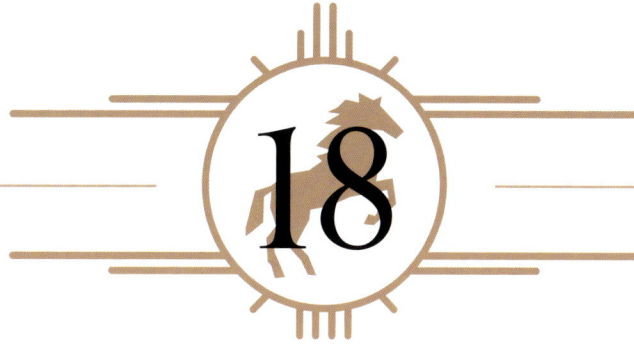

FIFTY SHADES OF BAY

T HE BAYS ARE SOME OF THE MOST BEAUTIFUL HORSES AT SKYDOG, and I'm happy to feature a few of them in this chapter. Little Jack Sparrow is one of my favorites but also, without a doubt, a favorite of our photographers. This Mustang had been "saved" with a group of young Mustangs from a kill pen when a "rescue" operation had fundraised for them and then kept the money and disappeared, leaving the horses at the pen.

As they had already been fundraised for once, people were having no luck raising more money, so we stepped in and worked with the incredible Mustang rescue Lifesavers, who would take the horses while we covered their bail, quarantine, and transport. We often do this, sometimes behind the scenes and sometimes publicly. If we know that the horses are going to a good place and will be adopted out with contracts and home checks, we are happy to help facilitate more rescues, as we can't take them all.

We paid for this group and moved them to our quarantine in Colorado, but tragically, after a couple of weeks, this little bay boy had a melting corneal ulcer that needed treatment by a vet. Luckily, he was young and open to being handled, and even though he'd never

been handled, our hauler Carla managed to get a halter on him and gentle him enough for the vet to see him. He needed a hospital and surgery, and I called around every equine hospital in the area until Colorado State University agreed to do the enucleation.

Jack did amazingly well, and we named him Jack Sparrow for his one-eyed pirate look and for his bravery during the process. He came to Oregon and finished his treatment at Bend Equine, handling the whole thing like a champ and behaving like he'd been tame his entire life. He finally came home to Skydog, where he stayed with a small bunch in a pen until he was turned out with a herd. He lacked confidence at first, but amazingly, our horse angel, Angel, stepped up, took him under her wing, and brought him into the herd,

OPPOSITE: *Jack Sparrow and friends*

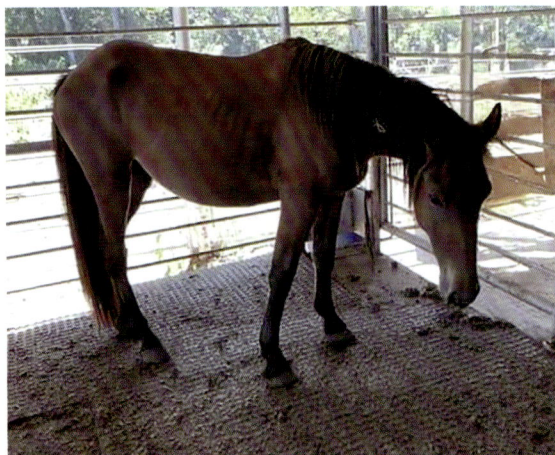
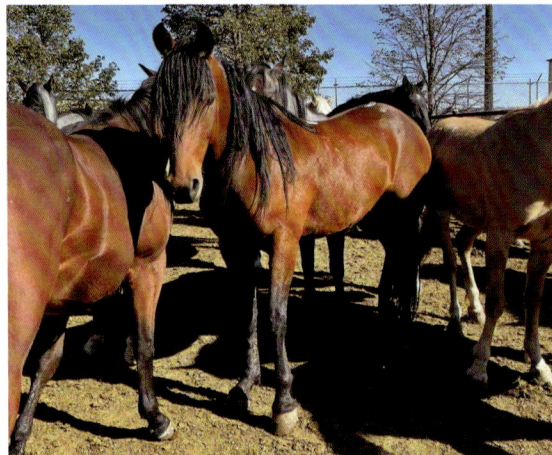

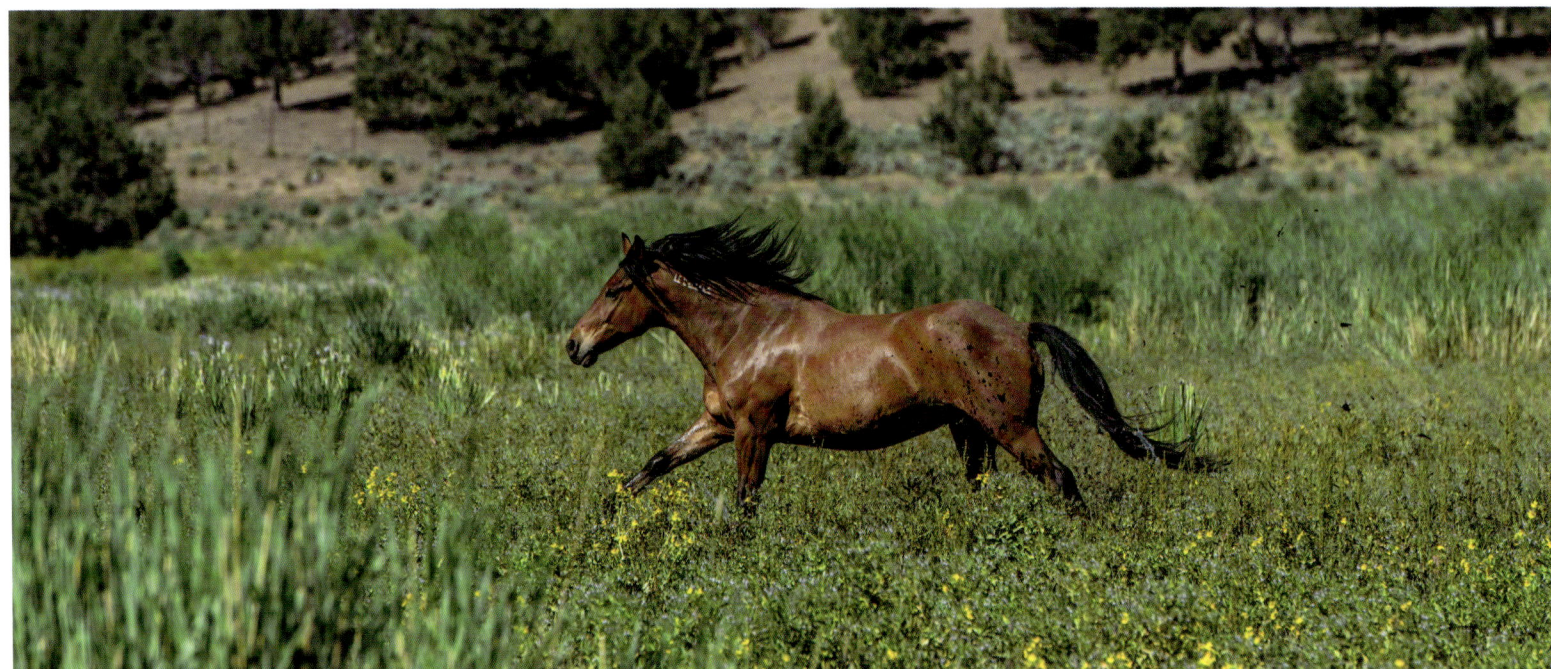

protecting him on his blind side and helping him make friends with the other youngsters, Skye and Scout. He's living his best life out there now, being a young lieutenant for Phoenix and still with his girl Skye and best friend Scout.

Drifter's story could not be more different, as he was a band stallion off the range who we spotted at the adoption event for Blue Zeus, one of the stars of our first book, *Wild Horses of Skydog*. While all the other older boys were staying away from people at the back of the small enclosures, he was right at the front eating all the alfalfa and rolling around in it and taking a nap, inches from people who he seemed to have no fear of. We had to save him for his personality alone. He was a deep mahogany bay, and we had no idea what a beauty he would blossom into once spring came.

Even though Drifter came to us alongside some flashy paints and Blue Zeus himself, he stood out as a gorgeous and somewhat friendly boy and came closer than any of the other wild boys when we were feeding every morning. Everyone fell in love with him, and he has lived up to his name, as Drifter would often wander away from the herd to explore and make new friends but always returned to his buddies once his drifting moods passed.

Gunsmoke was one of the saddest stories I had ever encountered. A photographer who took pictures out on South Steens HMA asked us to take this horse; otherwise, he was going to shoot him, simply because he didn't make a good saddle horse. I have never received such a direct and upsetting email, and I clarified in writing that he meant what he said in all seriousness, and he did. We said yes to save his life, and this was a well-known horse and

TOP LEFT & ABOVE: *Jack Sparrow* • TOP MIDDLE: *Neo* • TOP RIGHT & OPPOSITE: *Drifter*

son of the most famous foundation stallion from the South Steens.

Gunsmoke had a different name on the range, but we changed it slightly because we had previously named a horse Gunner, and we wanted him to have a new name for his new life, leaving all the negativity behind him. He is a gorgeous bay with white socks and is partially wild but loves cookies and strokes, and I always make sure to find him in the herd and give him some loving. He's a great horse, and I'm glad we could take him in.

Neo was an owner surrender who we took in for a #givingtuesday save, as he's originally from Warm Springs, Oregon, and we love to bring them home. Neo was run through Billings Livestock Auction and bought by a notorious kill buyer and ended up at Fabrizius's Colorado kill pen, unhandled and very wild. Thankfully, a good rescue saved him and went to great lengths to gentle and train him. Neo had been sent to some of the best-known and most successful trainers to help him transition to domestic life, but he didn't want to give up his wildness.

A lot of private funds went into his training, and they only reached out to us once they exhausted all possibilities, which we really appreciated. He now runs in the boys' herd with Commander, Rango, Cavalier, and Memphis, his best friend. His small herd is very popular and contains some of our most requested wild boys, so thankfully, we get to see a lot of them. Neo the bay—another breathtaking beauty of a Mustang.

OPPOSITE: *Neo* • ABOVE: *Gunsmoke* • PAGES 216 & 218: *Jack Sparrow* • PAGE 217: *Neo* • PAGE 219: *Drifter*

skydogsanctuary

Jack Sparrow

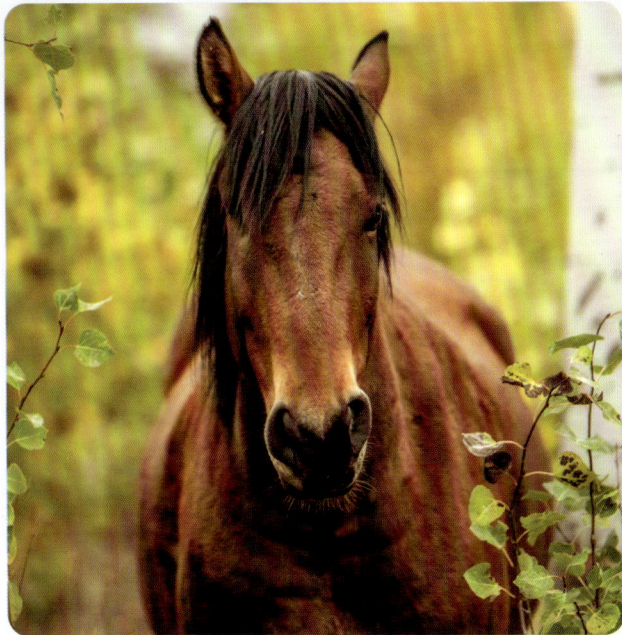

Jack Sparrow is home. 🖤 This little two-year-old baby was another one of the discarded AIP Mustangs that someone took the incentive money for and then dumped. This adorable little boy was going to a wild horse rescue in California with four others. Sadly, an ulcer in his eye caused him to have to be removed, so we said yes to him coming here, and we are sending another lucky save in his place next week. I can't wait to see them arrive at Lifesavers and start their new journey for real. Jack had his eye removed and has been at Bend Equine for the past week. He came home yesterday, and we all fell in love. He truly is the poster boy for a wild horse who was unhandled, but all his instincts and senses told him that these humans were trying to help him and that he needed to let them. Mustangs are, without doubt, the most incredibly smart horses, and their will and instinct to survive surpass all else. This little wild boy gentled for handling, vet visits, surgery, and aftercare so he could live and let people help him get better. He is a clever cookie, and we are so glad the heavens aligned and he ended up with us. I can't wait to see him out, running and playing with the other young ones. Out of the sixty or so horses we did manage to place and find soft landings for, there is one more coming to us soon, who you'll meet, but for now, welcome home, Jack Sparrow. You little pirate Mustang, you can stop sailing the high seas now. You, my friend, are finally home. ❤️

RIGHT: *Gunsmoke*

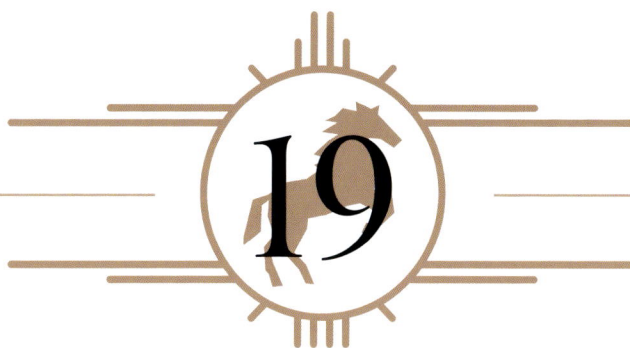

19

Roany Ponies

Our roans are sensational. It's like having four different horses, as they change colors with the seasons and are almost unrecognizable as roans in the cold months, wearing their winter darks. Our little Baby Blue came to us thanks to his better-known father and brothers. He is the son of Blue, the famous stallion who is still wild and free on the Pine Nut Mountain Range in Nevada. His brothers are Samson and Jet, who we saved as a family when they were bait-trapped by the BLM one Thanksgiving weekend.

Baby Blue was at the BLM corrals and saved by a woman who also had named him out on the range. She had boarded him for training with another woman, and somehow, the relationship had soured, and she was now upset at the small space he was in and worried about him. So we said we would take him, as he looked pretty miserable in the videos she sent, and we wanted to bring him home to family. Even if he couldn't live with them, he could see them over the fence.

So little Baby Blue came to Skydog. I say "little" because all the Pine Nut ponies are small, as they were descended from pit ponies that miners used to take down the coal mines. They were bred to be smaller to fit down the low passages, where they would then bring the coal

to the surface in carts. There was no such life for Baby Blue, but he ended up captured and in not such a great spot, so we went to pick him up.

He is such a funny little boy and sweet as anything, other than his habit of picking fights with horses twice his size and strength. The first year he was with us, I couldn't count the number of bite marks he had on his butt because once he realized he was outmatched, he was nipped at as he ran away. While he loved being wild, he eventually transitioned to "wild with cookies on the side." He joined the big boys' herd and made friends with Driggs, who I think felt sorry for him at first, but now he's a much-loved and accepted member of the gang.

Memphis was a great rescue. We first saw him when

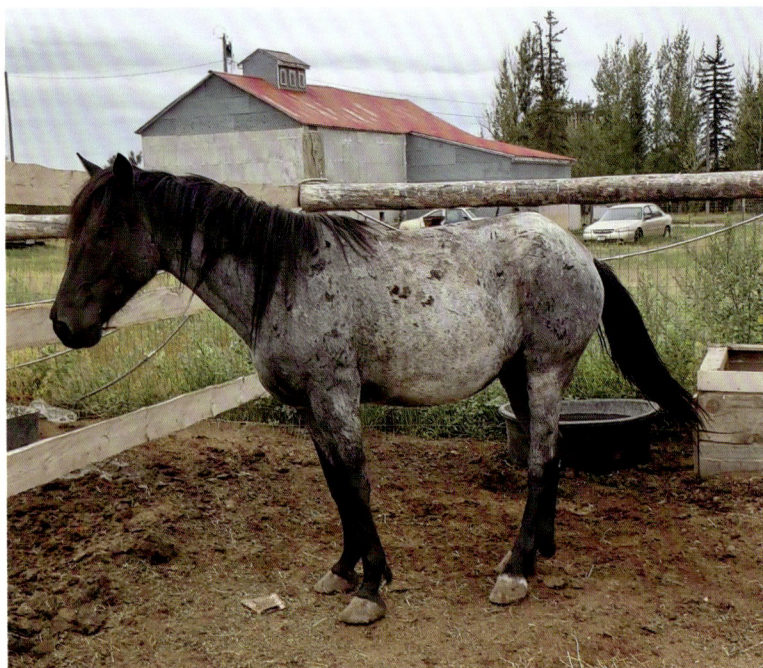

we went to pick up Cricket and Cedar from the corrals. He was in with some trainer returns, and the adoption staff pointed out the massive chunk missing from his hip, which resulted in the immortal words, "We might come back for you."

When our #givingtuesday was successful, we said we would go to the corrals and get one more horse. I looked back for the video and, luckily, hadn't deleted it because there was Memphis. I named him for Elvis's birthplace, and sure enough, we went back for him at the end of the year.

After we got Memphis home, a woman who had adopted him initially wrote to us to tell his story. She told us that while she had made great progress with him, she could not trim his feet. She kept working on it and tried to go at a pace that suited him without going too fast. Unfortunately, the BLM seized Memphis because she could not give him hoof care, which I found sad but also understood. She had gone to the corrals many times to see "her horse" and repeatedly asked them to let her know where he went. Well, he came to Skydog, and when I heard the woman's story, I told her that she could see him whenever she liked.

It was such an emotional visit when she came, as she quite clearly loved him very much. He recognized her immediately and trotted over to say hello. She brought a ton of carrots and cookies, and I must admit, I shed a tear for the bond they had and the love they shared. This really wasn't a case of a horse needing to be taken away. Compliance checks are irregular and so hit and miss, but done properly, they would help protect more horses.

Memphis became best friends with Neo, and they are usually together in the boys' herd with Commander. Even in his winter browns, I can recognize him by the big chunk out of his hip, which was likely the result of a mountain lion attack when he was young and still wild. He's a lovely boy and was certainly gentled well by his former adopter, and she's welcome to come anytime to visit him.

Our last roan is one I couldn't leave out because he is, without a doubt, one of the most beautiful horses I have ever seen, second only to his dad in beauty and elegance: the blue roan pinto son of Zeus, Huckleberry himself. His story is legendary and has been told often, but he is rarely featured just for himself, so let's recall how Huck came to Skydog.

I went to the BLM Corrals at Cañon City in Colorado to search for Blue Zeus's family members, hoping to find any of his mares or babies who were rounded up with him and return them to him. There were eight big pens full of mares and babies, and we went through each one, looking at hundreds of horses and trying desperately to match one with the photographs I had clutched in my hands. By pen seven, I was losing hope and was praying for a sign when a tiny foal ran up to me, not away as all the others were doing, and skidded to a halt in front of me.

I said, "Hello, my huckleberry friend," and was shocked when I realized this foal had identical markings to Blue Zeus: high white socks, blue roan coat, even the same white mark under his mane. It felt like a sign to keep looking, and I wrote down his mother's

ABOVE LEFT & OPPOSITE: *Baby Blue* • ABOVE RIGHT: *Memphis*

number, just in case I couldn't find any of them, as this could probably be Blue Zeus's son.

Unbelievably, in the next and last pen, I found three of Blue Zeus's mares, two of his older children, who were rounded up with them, and two newborn babies. I was stunned and overjoyed. I didn't think about the foal again until our hauler contracted COVID-19, and we found someone else to haul our horses home. They had a bigger trailer and had a compartment empty, so my mind went back to that tiny soul and his mother. I pulled out their numbers and added them. It was the best decision of my life.

Whether or not Huckleberry is genetically Blue Zeus's offspring, to us, he is his son in every sense of the word. His father raised and taught him how to be a Mustang colt, growing up with the best dad in the world. He is the only other gelding in the herd and loves his sisters and new friends. I love him for all the joy and hope he brought me that day, inspiring me to keep going and giving me a God nod that our mission was about to be completed in a way we could never have dreamed. Ten horses came home thanks to Blue Zeus and that trip to the corrals that day, and they are still running free at Skydog.

THIS SPREAD: *Huckleberry* • OVERLEAF: *Memphis*

skydogsanctuary

Memphis

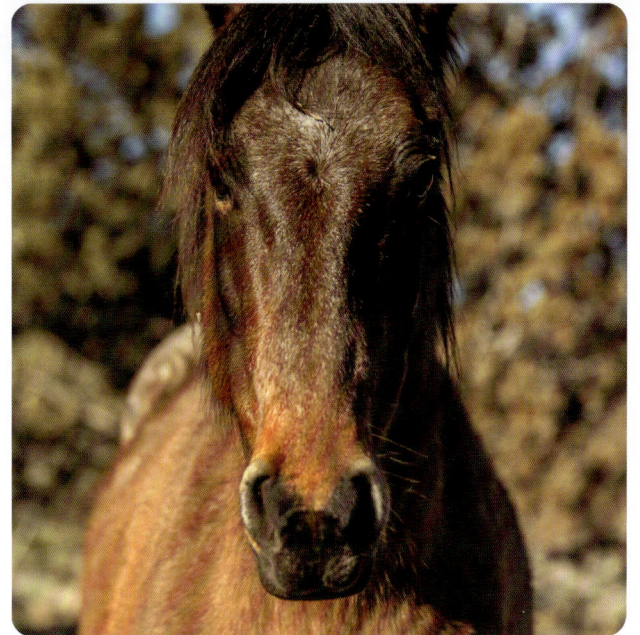

I left off yesterday with Memphis looking around him in awe at his new surroundings, wondering how he had got into a metal box at the corrals and ended up here. 🧡🧡 But what we all wanted to see was Memphis meet his new herd mates, Commander, Rango, and Neo. And here we have it. 🧡

Once he recovered from the shock of being here, he realized that horses were in with him. He trotted and then ran toward them, being careful on the slippery ground as he approached Neo, who was trotting over to meet him. Neo gave his signature double pound to show dominance, and Memphis took it well and then trotted to meet the other two boys. No drama there and quiet acceptance and a welcome before Memphis ran back to check out the rest, now that he'd said his hellos. I know it's muddy and the horses are wet, but nothing detracts from the beauty of new horses being greeted by others who feel quite at home. I'm sure they smell the corrals on the newbie and reassure in their calm manner that there is nothing to worry about now. This place is good, the people are kind, and the food is great. And nobody asks you to do anything at all that might be scary. 🧡

And so it begins—another life begun again in love and compassion thanks to all of you who donated on #givingtuesday, cheered us on, and made this possible. 🧡 It never gets less meaningful or fails to fill my eyes with tears, once I put down my phone to take it all in. 🧡 "Thank you" never seems to be enough, and soon the mud will be gone and these guys will go out, and I'm going to go visit them daily still and keep you updated on their progress.

20

THE THREE MUSKETEERS

THE BOOK WOULDN'T BE COMPLETE without including these three glorious horses. Their trio began with a kill pen horse named Tank, whose story is heartbreaking. I received a note from a girl who brokers kill pen horses, and she asked me to take this senior Mustang, as "he was too fat and ugly for anyone to save" and looked like a walking vet bill. No horse should ever be called names, and I didn't see what she saw at all. I saw a chunky dun with teddy bear ears that looked small compared to his large frame. He had the sweetest face, and I said yes without even thinking about it. Having been called a few names in my time, I immediately empathized with Tank and paid his bail.

We brought him home to Oregon and expected to find all kinds of things wrong with him, like Cushing's and metabolic issues, but tests revealed none of that, so we surmised that someone had just been feeding him a ton of sugar. The only human contact he would tolerate was getting handed a cookie, so all the signs were there. Maybe someone cared for him but didn't know that they should not give him so many treats, and the only way they could interact with him was to stretch their arm out with a sweet treat. He did turn out to have one painful issue with a very long name: equine odontoclastic tooth resorption and hypercementosis (EOTRH). We had the vet remove his front teeth, and he's been fine ever since.

For the longest time, Tank didn't bond with a particular horse and was always part of a group of guys but without that special friend—until we got a call about a very special horse named Sinatra. Our good friend Jamie Baldanza, whose photographs grace this book, reached out about a horse she had photographed and filmed a lot in the wild. He was a blue-eyed boy with a seriously wonky blaze who stood out in the wide-open spaces of Twin Peaks HMA, where she filmed most of her documentary *Wild Lands Wild Horses*.

OPPOSITE: *Sinatra and Tank*

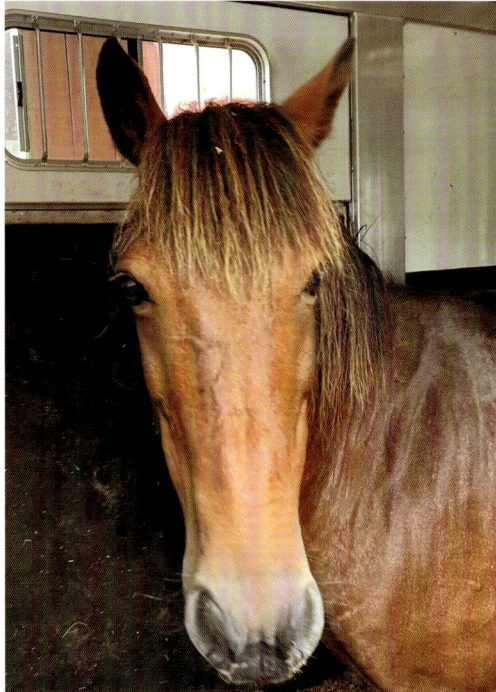

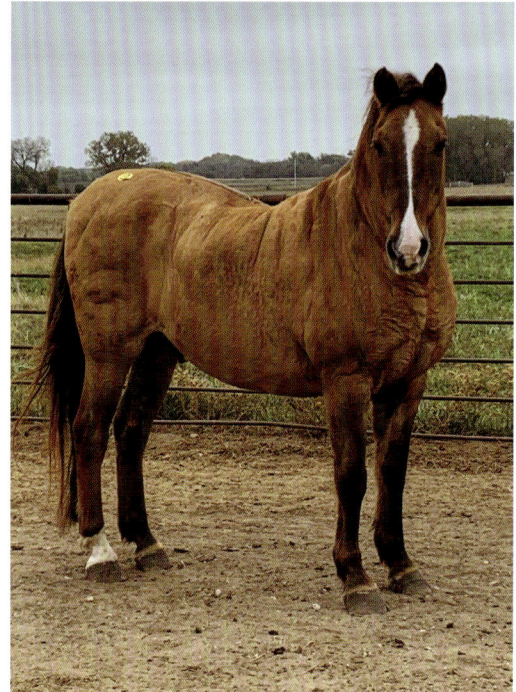

She had just discovered that Sinatra, or Blue Eyes as he was also known, had been captured by a rancher who lived on the outskirts of public lands that comprised the Herd Management Area Sinatra lived on. This rancher had effectively bait-trapped a wild horse by luring him into a pen with alfalfa and then had bred him to his mares and called the BLM to take him away. That ended his wild life, and all those who knew him were devastated to find out they would never see him out on the range again.

But a group of intrepid women didn't give up so easily. They started calling the corrals at Litchfield in California, where he had been taken, and begged for his release and asked to adopt him. Sadly, they were told he had already been shipped to long-term holding and wasn't available. They somehow managed to get a sympathetic BLM employee on the phone who told them he could be pulled off the load in Nebraska and held there to be picked up.

Jamie called me and asked me if I would take him early on in the rescue, and thinking there wasn't a chance they could get him released when he had already shipped, I said yes. Well, wasn't I wrong? Suddenly, we were arranging transport for him to get from Nebraska to Oregon and freedom. Sinatra was in a terrible state when he reached us, and it broke my heart to see this once wild and free, proud and healthy horse reduced to a skinny, shivering wreck. We called the vet as an emergency, and she came to examine him in the chute. He was very sick with severe kidney disease and pneumonia. If he were tame, he would be hospitalized, but we had to do his treatment in the chute, with an IV flooding his body with fluids to try to turn this around. We believe the stress of capture, then gelding, and so many hauls in a short period badly compromised his health.

Often, horses won't drink on hauls, which can lead to dehydration, which is hard on the kidneys. Sinatra had to be in the chute several times a day and evening to be given fluids, and it was remarkable, some would say miraculous, that this utterly wild horse stood patiently for over two hours at a time to receive the lifesaving treatment he needed. He was such a good patient, and slowly but surely, his health improved. While being kept close to the barn, he made friends with a little Chincoteague pony called Neptune, who makes up the third part of these three musketeers.

We received an email from the Chincoteague Fire Department, which manages a herd of wild ponies on an island off the coast of Virginia. The story of this herd of ponies is legendary and strongly suggests they are descendants of the survivors of a Spanish galleon that wrecked off the coast of Assateague Island. The breed was made famous by the *Misty of Chincoteague* novels, written by Marguerite Henry and published in 1947. I grew up reading and loving those books and would dream about running away to this island where the wild ponies lived. Never in my wildest dreams did I think I would one day meet and adopt one.

The email explained that they had rounded up an older stallion named Neptune, as he was infertile but had a large band of mares

ABOVE LEFT & OPPOSITE: *Sinatra*• ABOVE MIDDLE: *Neptune* • ABOVE RIGHT: *Tank*

that weren't breeding. They had removed him to balance the population and keep it healthy, and he was now living at the fairground nearby. They had hoped to gentle him, but he was very wild, and they were now searching for a sanctuary for him with a chute and experience with handling wild horses. We said yes—how could we say no to the stuff dreams were made of for this horse-crazy little girl living so far away in Cobham, a village in Surrey, England? He made the long journey to us after being gelded.

Neptune did not find a friend when we turned him out, so we brought him back in, and he ended up being put with Sinatra and Tank. The three bonded when they were turned out with a big herd. These three amigos figured out they would get the hay first if they waited right by the gate, so they formed a little wait-by-the-gate club, which was born of their love of food. Every day, when I drove in and out of the ranch, I saw little Neptune with his pony belly waiting for food with his two best friends. It made me happy whenever I saw him.

After a year of living in that pasture, we turned Neptune and his best friends out on the lower ranch to give them more space and adventures together, but they never really joined the big herd and stuck with each other. If you saw one, you knew the other two weren't far away. We noticed in late summer that Neptune had started losing weight, and we brought him in to give him extra food and care. When he didn't gain weight, we called the vet out to examine him.

It absolutely shattered my heart when he continued to lose weight, and I would go sit with him for hours, willing him to eat and throwing his favorite cookies on the ground at his feet, hoping they would help. We watched him deteriorate, and none of us wanted him to suffer, so a few weeks after we first brought him back into the barn, we made the very difficult decision to let him pass away peacefully under vet recommendation and supervision. I am not sure I have ever totally recovered from losing our Chincoteague pony, but I still see Tank and Sinatra together in their herd, sometimes standing by the gate, and in my mind's eye, I see Neptune there with them, too. I hope he's running the beaches of his island again, back with his family and friends and the sandy lands he called home.

OPPOSITE: *Sinatra* • ABOVE & OVERLEAF: *Neptune* • PAGES 238–239: *Tank* • PAGES 240–241: *Neptune*

If you are on Patreon, you will have already met Neptune and read how much he means to me. I'm sure my love of horses and starting a sanctuary for wild ones was born out of pure childhood love. When I was little, I devoured books like *Black Beauty*, cried when a horse died in a movie or on TV, and ran through the woods behind my home to visit with my neighbor's horses until I had one of my own. Today is a very special day because my absolute favorite book was *Misty of Chincoteague*, a true story about a band of wild horses who lived free on an island after the Spanish galleon they were on shipwrecked. I must have read that book about the Phantom and Pied Piper and little Misty a hundred times. I couldn't believe all these many years later that I received a letter from the volunteer fire department of Chincoteague asking us to take an older stallion (now a gelding) who couldn't adjust to domestic life and was sterile. They asked us to take him so he could have his freedom back, as he had lived on a remote part of the island, barely accessible to people. They generously donated his haul, and we said yes. Today, he's on his way, and it's truly full circle to be able to give one of these special horses in need a soft landing. I have to thank everyone on Patreon for this, as they made it possible for Neptune just by being on there. If you aren't on Patreon it's so easy to join at www.patreon.com/skydogsanctuary, and then you, too, will be helping Neptune and all of our horses. A little Chincoteague pony is coming to Oregon, and the seven-year-old inside me is bursting with happiness today. I dreamed of going to this island and seeing the ponies, and now one is in need, and we are going to honor *Misty of Chincoteague*, the book that planted the seed of this sanctuary, which has saved so many wild horses. I would love to hear if anyone else has read the book or visited the island. I love that at the auction, the highest bids are on the babies who are "buybacks" and get to return to the island to be free. Sweet Neptune, our grass might not taste as salty or sweet, but, boy, you are coming to Skydog. ❤️

21

THE BEST OF FRIENDS

THE PHOTOGRAPH *(overleaf)* NEEDS NO WORDS and is one of my favorites in this book. Finn, Tristan, and Hemingway the donkey came to Skydog to shine a bright light on the emergence of fake rescues exploiting and continuing the suffering of horses and donkeys in the slaughter pipeline. They came to remind everyone to be careful where donations are sent to "save" a horse. Many of these new social-media-driven places have ill intentions, and they are mostly there to become Instagram famous or to make money by exploiting horses and holding them ransom.

This story is becoming more and more common. Groups on Facebook fundraise for a horse and then send it to a place nobody has ever been or seen in person, without any contract or way to get the animal back if it turns bad. Or mass bailers use these places as a dumping ground for horses and donkeys they heavily fundraise for with a lot of tears and then never check on them again. There have been so many over the years, and I have seen the devastating outcomes for animals sent there who die of starvation or are later shipped to slaughter anyway after being given no care for months.

Finn and Tristan, with their donkey buddy Hemingway, were sent to a terrible "rescue" in Texas, which is a state where animal protection laws seem nonexistent, based on their lack of action, regardless of the amount of evidence animals are suffering and dying at this house of horror. Skydog had come close to saving Finn and

his bonded friend Arrow when he had originally been advertised by a kill pen. But we eventually had to rescue him when he was again sent back to auction after surviving starvation at this terrible place.

Their story is important, but more than anything else, they represent a common story of many of the horses at our sanctuary. They went to hell, nearly didn't survive, and were saved by Skydog. And the pride and happiness it gives us to lovingly provide them with care, love, respect, and kindness means the world to us. The stories are different but all the same. I wish these wild horses had all remained on the range, living peaceful, wild lives with their families on their homeland. But when that is ripped away from them, we always want to be here to provide protection and a soft landing for them. Thanks to you and many others, we have been able to save hundreds of wild horses from the most terrible fates.

OPPOSITE: *Finn and Tristan* • OVERLEAF: *Hemingway, Finn, and Tristan with Clare* • PAGES 246–247: *Finn* • PAGES 248–249: *Cookie and friends*

My new best friends. Handsome heroes Finn and Tristan walk up to me like we've known each other forever, and somehow, it feels like we have.

When I first saw that Finn had gone to an unknown new rescue, I was worried he'd been rescued alone without his bonded friend, but I was relieved when I saw his friend had joined him. How wrong could I have been?

As updates were infrequent, I was shocked at the huge number of branded, unhandled mustangs this place was taking with no following or donor support. I saw a couple of photos of Finn and his friend, and the next thing I saw was a video of Finn standing alone, and somehow, I knew. They were both thin when they'd gone there, and seniors with few teeth don't have the ability to live off the land. By then, a lot of concerned people and groups had started worrying about horses sent there. And the whole nightmare began in earnest, and never in my wildest dreams did I think it would take another year to finally fulfill the promise I made to this beautiful boy and say the words, "Welcome to Skydog." But now he's home, and when I look into his kind, gentle eye, I see and feel so much of what he endured. We looked for a brand on his neck, but he's so old it's faded away, and all you can see is the big U at the end of where it was. So we've no idea how old he was or where he's from. And maybe that's the way it should be—a mystery. I feel like Finn is an avenging angel who came to us to tell his story and speak about what he saw and what he went through. And maybe his story can be an education so that these horses stop ending up in places like he landed in, because I can tell you, it's not the only place like that. Over the years, I've seen it more times than I would like to share, and often, the horses are deceased by the time I see pictures of them. I just won't stay silent anymore. Finn, Tristan, and Hemingway deserve better and more than that and for us to bear witness. And maybe they're with us to shine a bright light on these dark places and bring change. But for now, they're home, they're safe, and they are so loved by thousands of people who care about them.

I am always reminded of Black Beauty's words in the final chapter of *Black Beauty* when I look at these horses and remember their past horrors and abuse: "My ladies have promised that I shall never be sold, and so I have nothing to fear; and here my story ends. My troubles are all over, and I am at home; and often before I am quite awake, I fancy I am still in the orchard at Birtwick, standing with my old friends under the apple-trees."

And on we go . . .

EPILOGUE
The Eight Things You Can Do to Help the Wild Horses of America

1 FOLLOW US ON SOCIAL MEDIA @skydogsanctuary, share our posts, and donate to our fundraisers to help us help more Mustangs in need. The more people who find out about and fall in love with wild horses, the better. The more we are supported, the more horses we can save.

2 CONTACT YOUR STATE REPRESENTATIVES, remind them how important the wild horses are to Americans, and ask them to cosponsor the Save America's Forgotten Equines (SAFE) Act, which would help stop the transport of wild horses across our borders to Mexico and Canada to be slaughtered.

3 VOLUNTEER AT A LOCAL HORSE RESCUE or offer your talents to a wild horse organization and work remotely to help in any way you can. At Skydog, we have some incredible people behind the scenes sending thank-yous, welcoming new patrons, taking photographs of our wild horses to share with the world, and donating items to our auctions to raise funds. There are many different ways you can get involved and help the cause.

4 CONTACT YOUR LOCAL MEDIA and ask them to run more stories about horse and donkey rescues or the wild horses and burros of America.

5 ADOPT A MUSTANG or encourage your knowledgeable, horse-loving friends to do so. Mustangs are the most incredible horses—smart, hardy, sure-footed, athletic, and soulful. You can rescue one from the slaughter pipeline easily, and the journey you will take with that horse (or donkey), learning how to gentle him and become his trusted friend and partner, is the greatest journey of self-discovery you can take.

6 Follow other reputable horse rescues and sanctuaries, and share and post about their mission and message to help raise awareness and educate others. We can all do a small part to change things for wild horses when enough people know about the issues and more get involved in the fight for their right to freedom.

7 Research the subject. There are many great organizations doing good work to educate people about our wild horses, including American Wild Horse Conservation (www.americanwildhorse.org).

8 Talk about wild horses. Whenever you can get into conversations about Mustangs and the issues they face, see if you can inform more people and inspire them to get involved. Tell them about Skydog Ranch and Sanctuary. Display our merchandise and stickers to provoke conversations about Skydog when you're out and about. All proceeds from the purchase of our merchandise go directly to maintaining the sanctuary and rescuing more wild horses (www.skydogranch.org).

ABOVE: *Horses at the pond*

ACKNOWLEDGMENTS

MY SINCEREST THANKS GO TO photographers Shannon Phifer, Scott Wilson, and Jamie Baldanza who took and donated beautiful pictures of the horses for this book, while out in remote locations in all weather. I am very grateful to Janelle Hight, who, on top of taking the very best care of all the horses, took some magical photographs that make the book extra special.

Thank you to American Wild Horse Conservation for their tireless work fighting for wild horses and burros and for fighting to end the adoption incentive program with us.

Steph K Equestrian for saving Atsa and bringing him to Skydog, thus giving him back his much-needed freedom in his home state.

Caroline from Horse Welfare Collective for finding Commander.

Lela Pena for adopting and sending Cruiser to us to be reunited with his mare and son, Jorja.

Our Crew of hard-working and dedicated staff, who work tirelessly to feed and care for the close to three hundred and fifty equines we have rescued.

My husband, Chris, without whom we would never have been able to start Skydog and make it the wonderful place it is today, where horses can be horses.

Our followers and supporters, who lift me up and keep me going with their amazing likes, comments, and emails when they're needed most—especially our patrons and sponsors, who make it possible to do this work and say yes to more horses and donkeys when needed.

Our amazing publisher, Martha Cook; designer, Iain R. Morris; and editor, Jan Hughes.

And finally, thank you to my special first Mustang, Buddy, and our first wild boy, Jackson, who both taught me so much about being of service, about Mustangs, about family, and about myself.

OPPOSITE: *Frostmoon* • OVERLEAF: *Blue Zeus* • PAGE 256: *Las Vegas*

Skydog Ranch & Sanctuary
would love to hear from you!

Please visit us at SKYDOGRANCH.ORG for more information
about the work we are doing and the ways you can get involved
to help wild horses and burros.

We invite you to follow the stories of our wild horse families
on Instagram and Facebook @SKYDOGSANCTUARY.

The movie *Blue Zeus* will be out in 2025, so follow @bluezeusthemovie
for more information on how to see the film.

T S

TRAFALGAR SQUARE

First published in 2025 by
TRAFALGAR SQUARE BOOKS
an imprint of The Stable Book Group
32 Court Street, Suite 2109
Brooklyn, New York 11201
www.TrafalgarBooks.com

Library of Congress Control Number: 2025940477
ISBN: 978-1-64601-276-3

PHOTOGRAPHS BY
Scott Wilson, Shannon Phifer, Jamie Baldanza &
Janelle Hight. Additional photographs of Atsa
by Steph K Equestrian.

All efforts have been made to locate the contributors and
to credit them with the appropriate copyright information.
Requests for changes will be considered by the publisher,
and any necessary corrections or revisions will be
amended in future printings.

Book & cover design by Iain R. Morris

Printed & bound in China
10 9 8 7 6 5 4 3 2 1

SKY DOG

RANCH